D1130056

This is the second of a series of books for 14–16-year-olds which set out to teach history through individuals, and which can be read and enjoyed as stories.

This book shows what life was like for a typical factory worker and his family a century ago. It tells the story of their day, from the time they got up in the morning until they went to bed at night, and is full of fascinating details about the clothes they wore, the food they ate, the work they did, and the way in which they lived and played. Among the many topics included are the work of the first of the new model unions, the setting up of Board schools after the Education Act of 1870 and the beginning of sanitary and housing reforms in the industrial towns.

The story is followed by a final chapter on regional and working-class variations in Victorian industrial society, which is suitable for general reading and discussion, and there is an appendix which contains many suggestions for follow-up work and projects. The book will appeal to all teachers who are interested in Victorian social and economic history, and particularly to the growing number who deal with local history.

Like the first highly-praised title in the series, *A Day in the Life of a Victorian Farm Worker*, by the same author, this book is based on a careful examination of many different nineteenth-century reports and records, archive material and reminiscences of those who lived at the time. The author, Frank E. Huggett, has written a large number of books on nineteenth-century history.

A Day in the Life of a Victorian Factory Worker

VICTORIAN DAY SERIES

VICTORIAN DAY SERIES: 2

A Day in the Life of A VICTORIAN FACTORY WORKER

FRANK E. HUGGETT

LONDON · GEORGE ALLEN & UNWIN LTD

Ruskin House   Museum Street

First published in 1973
Second impression 1976

This book is copyright under the Berne Convention. All rights are
reserved. Apart from any fair dealing for the purpose of private
study, research, criticism or review, as permitted under the Copyright
Act, 1956, no part of this publication may be reproduced, stored in a
retrieval system, or transmitted, in any form or by any means,
electronic, electrical, chemical, mechanical, optical, photocopying,
recording or otherwise, without the prior permission of the copyright
owner. Enquiries should be addressed to the publishers.

© George Allen & Unwin (Publishers) Ltd, 1973

ISBN 0 04 942112 3 hardback
       0 04 942113 1 paper

Filmset in 12 on 13 point Baskerville and printed
Offset Litho in Great Britain by Cox & Wyman Ltd,
London, Fakenham and Reading

Contents

Illustrations

The illustrations are reproduced by kind permission of the following: nos 1, 2, 10, 12 and 22, the Greater London Council; no. 3, Harry Milligan, A.R.P.S., A.M.I.R.T.; no. 6, the Institution of Mechanical Engineers; nos 4, 5, 7–9, 11, 13–21, the Trustees of the British Museum.

Preface

This book attempts to show what life was like for a factory worker and his family a hundred years ago. It reconstructs one day in the life of Bill Boddington, his wife, and their children, and describes what they did from hour to hour—at work, in the home and at school.

Although few factory workers have left a written record of their day-to-day life, details of how they lived are to be found in many contemporary reports, articles, and books; in archives and museums; in reminiscences of those who lived at the time; and in modern research into the Victorian age. It is upon these sources that this account is based.

Most of the book consists of a simple narrative and descriptive account, which is suitable for individual or group study. It is hoped that this approach will help to bring the past alive and will also stimulate the growing study of local history. Many points in the text can be used as springboards for local investigation of various aspects of Victorian industrial life. Some suggestions are contained in an appendix.

Although local history can provide an excellent and exciting introduction to historical method, the results have to be set in a wider national context if they are not to result in some distortion. The differences in life styles between various sections of the Victorian working classes and some of the main industrial developments before and after the 1870s are dealt with briefly in a final chapter. It is suggested that this could be most usefully studied in a group.

1. MORNING

Tap, tap, tap! Bill Boddington stirred uneasily in bed, somewhere between dreaming and waking. There were a few muffled shouts from the house next door followed by the sound of wooden-soled clogs clacking along the paved street. Bill woke up and realized that it had been no dream, but the sound of the 'knocker-up' waking his neighbour by rattling a long wooden pole against his bedroom window. It was 5.30 on a cold autumn morning —time to get up. Bill got out of bed and padded across the bare boards to a chair in the corner of the room. It was dark but he did not light the candle, so that his wife would go on sleeping.

Still wearing the thick check shirt and heavy socks that he had slept in, he groped around on the chair until he found his corduroy trousers and put them on. Then he put on his waistcoat, made of the same material as the trousers, and his jacket, and bent down to lace up his shoes. Opening the bedroom door, he walked through the smaller bedroom in which his five-year-old son, George, and his four-year-old daughter, Sarah, were sleeping, and went on down the bare, narrow staircase into the kitchen.

It was a little warmer downstairs than it was in the bedroom, which had no fireplace or other means of heating. Bill walked over to the 'kitchener' —a small, cast-iron kitchen range with an oven at the side—and warmed his hands by the embers of the dying fire. He lit a candle. It wasn't worth-while lighting the oil lamp as he wouldn't be in the kitchen very long. Opening the oven door, he took out the tin teapot that his wife had left there the previous night. He went into the scullery and returned with a mug containing a little milk and some sugar, and poured out a cup of tea. The tea was warm, but tasted bitter. He added some more sugar, but still shivered a little as he drank it down. Through the thin walls, which divided the houses, he could hear the sounds of the weaver and his two older daughters moving around next door, as they, too, got ready to go to work.

When he had finished his tea he opened the front door which led directly into the street. He lived in a row of terrace cottages, built back to back with a row of identical houses in the next street. None of them had backyards, and there were no front gardens either, only a narrow, roughly-paved court flanked by an eight-foot-high brick wall. There was not a tree or a flower to be seen. The court was shut off at one end by a huge blank wall, which

A London court, with housewives huddled in the corner and lines for hanging
out the washing. This photograph was taken in 1890

a stranger might not have recognized as the back wall of another row of
houses unless he had noticed the small pairs of chimney pots on top. Although
the houses had been built only twenty years before, they were so grimed with
soot and so shabby, that they looked as though they must have been part of
Loomtown for a century.

A row of three privies served the nine houses in the row. Bill walked over
to one; its door was hanging open at an angle because the bottom hinge
was broken and the landlord had never bothered to repair it. Inside, there
was nothing but a wooden seat with a wooden pail beneath it, made out of
half an old paraffin cask. It was cold and dark inside and he didn't stay
there any longer than he had to.

When he went back into the house, he got the ashtub out of the little
recess under the stairs and put it out into the street to await collection. He
blew out the candle. Then he put on his cap and woollen muffler and, with
the thinner jacket that he wore in the factory rolled up under his arm, he

set out for work. He wore the same clothes to the factory, winter and summer. He had no overcoat, so that when it was raining or snowing he arrived wet through to the skin, even though he lived only five minutes' walk away. Most of the men lived close to the factory; but a few of them had a mile or more to walk.

Bill went through the little archway which led out of the court in which he lived. There was never any breeze or air in the court, which was always warm in winter and stifling in summer. It felt much colder in the chill, raw air of the open street and he walked along quickly, his head downcast. His hands were half-clenched, not only because he felt cold, but also through a lifetime's habit of gripping hammers, chisels and files at his work. The top half of the little finger on his right hand was missing; very few men or women escaped some form of injury in the factories where they worked. Sometimes there were dreadful accidents. Earlier that year one man had been killed and six others seriously injured when the fly-wheel of a machine had broken at the big ironworks in the town. And only last month three men had been scalded to death in an escape of steam at one of the coal mines.

It was still dark; the sky was covered by heavy yellowish clouds so that not a star could be seen. The only light came from the gas lamps which spluttered and popped at the street corners. From time to time a flame shot up into the sky from the furnace of the big ironworks in the eastern part of the town. And in the distance a brick kiln glowed red in the gloom. Bill walked on under a railway bridge. Just at that moment a goods train rumbled overhead, its engine spitting out showers of sparks. Great clouds of black smoke curled down in billows over the parapet of the bridge. As he walked through the thick, black smoke Bill coughed and tried to rub the soot out of his eyes. The smoke gave him a feeling of tightness in his chest and he felt a sudden stab of pain which made him wince. He seemed to be getting these pains more frequently all the time; he didn't know what caused them.

As the smoke cleared, Bill could see the lights of the workhouse directly ahead. A huge, prison-like building, it had been built twelve years before to accommodate 1,000 people. Built on the summit of a hill, it seemed to dominate the whole town, a constant reminder of the fate that awaited the sick, the ill, the workless. Everyone in the town knew what went on inside. Children were taken away from their mothers; men were separated from their wives. The meals consisted of nothing but bread and porridge, or bread and gruel, with meat and a few rotten potatoes for variety on Mondays and Thursdays. It was the fear and shame of ending their lives in the work-house that got men and women out of bed so early and kept them hard at work all day, sometimes to eight or ten o'clock at night.

The streets were already full of silent figures in their dark, sombre clothes

15

marching past the shuttered shops to the mills and the factories. Most of the women were wearing aprons, black shawls over their heads, and clogs with wooden soles. A number were carrying babies which they would leave with some old woman who lived near the mill, returning to her house during the breakfast and dinner breaks to feed it. Even the younger women looked old and tired, with great care-worn eyes in their pale faces. There were a number of young 'half-timers' of ten or eleven among the crowds, dressed in thin, shabby clothes and vainly trying to rub the grit and the sleep from their eyes. They worked in the mills in the morning and went to school in the afternoon.

Some of the men were dressed in the same way as Bill Boddington, but a larger number wore older, shabbier clothes which had been much patched and repaired. Many of them were wearing clogs. There was no laughter or smiles, and even people who worked in the same factory scarcely spoke to each other. The only sound was the shuffling of boots and shoes, the clacking of clogs on the cobbled streets, and the sudden bursts of coughing and spitting as the grime and soot irritated someone's throat.

Bill Boddington, who was thirty-three, was a short man, barely five feet three inches tall. He had bright staring eyes and his pale face was streaked with grime and dirt. He worked as a fitter in a factory which made steam engines. His father had worked in the same factory before him. Bill could handle the tools of his trade as well as any man; he never touched a drink at work; he was never late; and he rarely missed a day's work, unless he was too ill to get out of bed. Both the factory owner, Mr Mark Ashworth, and the foreman, Mr Robert Lampard, thought highly of him, and Bill had some hopes that in the not too distant future he might be promoted foreman when Mr Lampard was too old for work.

It wasn't long before Bill and a few other men left the crowd of work-people and turned off down the side street which led to their factory. About halfway along the street a wooden board had been fixed outside the ground-floor window of a terrace house, where an old woman sold steaming mugs of hot coffee for $\frac{1}{2}$d. There were only one or two shabbily-dressed men standing by the coffee stall and Bill walked past them without a glance. Only common labourers ever patronized the coffee stall, or bought herrings or pies from the women outside the factory gates. He walked on more briskly towards the factory, which was situated at a street corner.

The firm had been founded fifty years before by old Mr Ashworth, the grandfather of the present owner. He had started his engineering business in a three-storey house which still formed part of the factory. As his business had prospered he had bought the houses on either side. Some of them were still used as storerooms, while others had been pulled down to make way for new buildings. The factory consisted of a disordered jumble of buildings made of different materials and built in different styles. Some roofs were flat, while others rose to a point; some buildings were three storeys high and others were only one. The only characteristic they had in common was their colour, for they had all been uniformly blackened by the soot and smoke which rose every day from the tall chimney above the foundry in one corner of the factory yard—and the other 200 factory chimneys in the town.

The original house was now used for offices; there the clerks and cashiers worked at their wooden desks in dark, low-ceilinged rooms. The family had moved out long ago to a large, but plain, mansion some three miles outside the town, where the present owner, Mr Mark Ashworth, still resided. It was built on a new road which led to a pleasant district of wooded hills and little valleys, where the Liberal M.P. for Loomtown also lived, in a vast mansion surrounded by a park.

Bill entered the factory through the large gateway next to the office. He took out his 'ticket'—a little round brass disc engraved with his name —and hung it on a board by the gatekeeper's shed. Every time he went into the factory he had to hand in his ticket, and he had to take it with him every time he left. If he lost his ticket he could be fined 6d. Timekeeping was very strict. At 6 a.m. the gatekeeper rang a bell and a few moments later he started to close the heavy wooden gates. No workmen were admitted after that. They had to wait until 8.30 a.m. before they could get in, which meant they 'lost a quarter', so that on Friday they would find a quarter of a day's pay had been deducted from their wages. If they lost too many quarters, the foreman would tell them off or even 'grass' them, that is send them home for the rest of the week without any wages. And if they were late too often they would find the gates closed to them for good, with, possibly, their name blacklisted by all the foremen in the town.

Bill walked on through the yard which looked just as untidy and dis-ordered as the exterior of the factory. There were big heaps of old, rusting iron and castings which Mr Ashworth refused to get rid of, as he believed that nothing was so good as the iron which had been made in the past. When he had a specially important job he would order some of the old iron to be melted down and used for it. Steam was already pouring out of the engine shed in that corner of the yard where the engine which drove all the machinery in the factory was situated. Next to it there was the foundry, where the crude iron was melted down so that it could be cast into the required shape. This was done in a small blast furnace about twelve feet high, which was filled with a mixture of coke and iron. A large fan was used to blow a draught of air into the furnace until the temperature became so high that the furnace threw off a dazzling white light. When the metal had melted it was drained off and carried away to the casting shed in pails or

17

An engineering works in 1863. The engine room is on the left and wooden staircases lead to the workshops in the upper storeys

The Nasmyth steam hammer, which was invented in 1839, allowed much larger forgings to be made. The operator stood on the platform on the left

18

ladles lined with sand so that they would not melt. The castings were made in moulds, filled with sand, which had been pressed into the required shape by wooden patterns. Some of the other parts were made by the smiths on their anvils in the forge on the opposite side of the yard. Larger parts were beaten out by a huge Nasmyth steam hammer. The Japanese minister had been very interested in this machine when he had visited the factory earlier in the year.

Bill climbed up the outside staircase at one end of a large building, which led to the workshops. He passed through the large pattern shop where the wooden patterns were made and stored for future use. Although the fitters and pattern makers were members of the same union, they did not mix very freely with each other. The fitters thought the pattern makers were stuck-up, as they called each other 'mister' while the fitters always used Christian names. At the end of the shop he slid open a big door which shut automatically behind him on its rollers. Bill entered a long rectangular room. The floor was covered with benches and machines, which were connected by leather belts to the pulley wheels on the shafts up above. There were lathes for making screws, gears and wheels; drilling machines; boring machines for making cylinders; and planing machines for cutting metal. Bill ducked under a leather belt, took off his jacket and hung it on a nail in the wall. He put on his working jacket which was made of thinner material so that it could be easily washed. Some of the other men were already at their machines or benches, while others were standing by the small round stove in the centre of the room. Bill walked over to the bench at which he worked. There was a rack holding files of different sizes, hammers, chisels, calipers for measuring and other kinds of tools. Although the room was full of machinery, much of his work, the most highly skilled, was still done by hand. After the parts of the engine had been cast, turned or forged, they went to the fitters. Sometimes with a chisel, but more often with a file or scraper, they worked away until the parts of the engine fitted each other exactly. A fitter's work needed patience, a steady hand, a good eye and a feeling for metal. The fitters looked upon themselves as the 'kings' of the factory. If they failed to make a dead fit, the finished engine would never run true, however much good work the other men had done.

Bill wouldn't have changed places with anyone else in the factory— except the foreman. In his shop there was very little noise, apart from the sound of the fitters scraping and filing at their benches and the whirring of the leather belts and the clickety-clack as the copper rivets passed over a pulley. But he scarcely noticed that. It was very different in the forge, where the force of the steam hammer was so great that the earth seemed to quake and the noise almost deafened you. Sometimes it was rather cold in his shop because several of the windows were broken; but he could bear the cold much

20 A fitting shop in a Leeds factory, similar to the one in which Bill Boddington worked. All the machines were driven by leather belts from the overhead pulleys

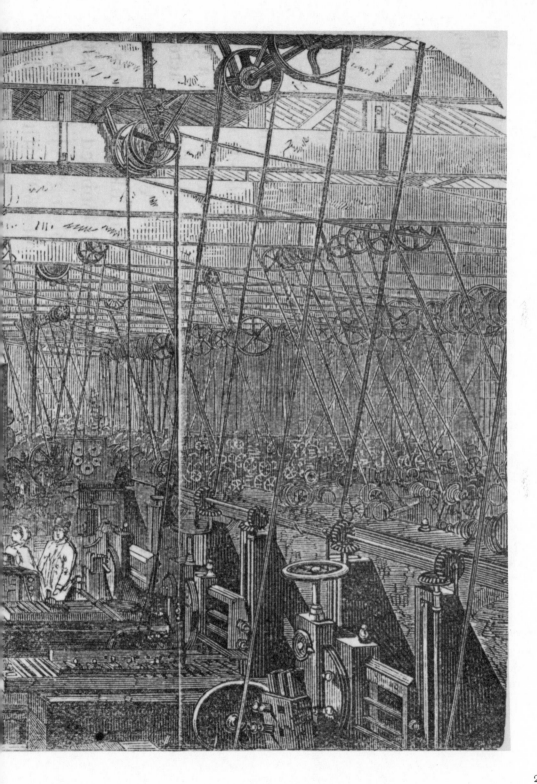

better than the heat of the furnace which was so sweltering that the foundry-men were too hot even in the depths of winter. And in his shop there were fewer fumes and less smoke, though even there it was impossible to escape entirely from the choking smell of sulphur and soot, which was never absent from the town completely, not even on Sundays when the factories and mills were closed.

There had been some changes since he'd first started work in the factory as a lad of twelve in 1852. The work had been more general then, as they'd made machinery of many different kinds; but now they specialized in making steam engines for other factories and coal mines. The engines were built entirely on the premises from the casting of the metal to the fitting and assembling of the finished parts. It had been quite different in the early days, when steam engines had been made on the site where they were to be used. The manufacturer had supplied the cylinder, the piston and the valves; other parts had been made by local blacksmiths; and the whole engine had been put together by a millwright. Bill's grandfather had been a millwright. He had travelled all over the north of England, building and repairing windmills and watermills, which were used to drive the machinery in the first factories. When steam engines had come in, his grandfather had turned his hand to making those. He had made a lot of money for those days, as he had earned over two guineas a week. But all of it had gone—on drink, so Bill had been told. Bill liked a drink himself, but he had seen and heard too much of the trouble it could cause ever to become a 'lushington', or heavy drinker, himself.

The shop had now filled up and a bell rang for the day's work to start. Soon the leather belts were whirling round, with the copper rivets clacking rhythmically over the wheels and pulleys; the turners were at their lathes and grindstones; the fitters at their benches filing and scraping engine parts held in metal vices. Bill had a labourer to help him lift heavy parts and fetch materials from the casting shop. He had worked with him for a number of years. Bill treated him fairly, but kept him at a distance. It didn't do to get too friendly with labourers. Some of the younger labourers were becoming a little too cheeky, even trying to join in the conversation when a group of skilled fitters were talking to each other. You had to keep them in their proper place unless you wanted trouble in the future. Bill had seen it happen many times. A fitter would get too friendly with his labourer and let him know too many secrets of their trade. Later, if there was a strike or a lock-out, the machines would be taken over by some of these 'knobsticks', which was what they called the men who were not skilled enough to become members of their union, the Amalgamated Society of Engineers. Afterwards, when the strike or lock-out was over, you could never get all of them off the machines again.

Bill also had an apprentice, a young lad of fourteen called John Smith, who ran errands and fetched tools for him. Bill was going to let him try his hand at using the tools after breakfast, though he hadn't told him yet.

They hadn't been working for very long before the first belt came off the pulley. It was always happening. You had to keep one eye on the belts and wheels all the time, for if you weren't careful your clothes could be caught in the straps and you could be maimed for life. There were shouts for 'Strappie' Marshall, as he was always called, and soon a little man smothered in oil and grease appeared, carrying a ladder. He climbed up among the shafts and pulleys and cut away the leather belt to take it away for repairs.

After they had been working for two hours the bell rang again, for breakfast. It was 8 a.m. The men who were staying in the factory made a rush for the stove where their tall, tin coffee cans were already heating. Others, like Bill, who lived near the factory, grabbed their jackets from the nails on the wall and hurried home. Some of the older men, like the foreman and some of the skilled craftsmen whose children were also earning money, left at a more leisurely pace to have their breakfast in an eating house or coffee shop opposite the factory gates, where an egg, bread and butter, and coffee could be bought for $4\frac{1}{2}$d.

It took Bill five minutes to get home and five minutes to get back again so that he had only twenty minutes for his breakfast. He hurried towards his house, where his family was already waiting for him. Mrs Boddington had got up at 7 a.m. to light the fire in the kitchener and build it up until it was blazing. Coal was cheap, as it was mined in the town, and they could afford to use it freely. She was just cutting the bread when Bill came in, slightly out of breath. His two young children, George and Sarah, were already sitting at the plain, square table in the kitchen. Bill went into the scullery and washed some of the powdered metal and oily dirt off his hands in the cold water from the tap, then went back into the kitchen. There was barely time for him to eat his breakfast of porridge and bread and butter, and to gulp down two mugs of fresh, hot tea, before it was time to set off for the factory again.

2. AT WORK

Bill left the house a couple of minutes earlier than usual; there was something happening in the factory after breakfast that he did not want to miss. The streets presented a more varied appearance than they had done two and a half hours before, when there had been nothing but the dense, silent crowds of men, women and children marching towards the mills and factories. The shutters of the shops had now been taken down and the assistants were sweeping the floor or dusting the counters, while the shopkeepers were arranging their stock or waiting on the doorstep for their first customers. A white-haired man drove past in his carriage and pair to the mill he owned. At the corner of a street a lamplighter was climbing up his ladder to turn out the gas light and to clean the glass. A fat, blowsy-looking woman with a wicker basket full of herrings walked down the street crying her wares. A number of married women were hurrying back to the mills after feeding their babies.

Bill was in good time. He walked comfortably towards a small crowd of men and boys waiting patiently at the factory gate. They were all dressed in their cleanest working clothes. Some of them were even wearing their Sunday 'best'—white corduroy trousers and waistcoats, smart jackets, red mufflers, and well-polished boots. There was usually a similar crowd at the gates, even on the wettest and coldest day, waiting for the foreman to return from breakfast to see if they could get a job. Bill glanced at the crowd wondering who would be taken on. There was one red-faced man who was an obvious 'lushington' and another man smoking a clay pipe. Bill knew that neither of them stood a chance; Mr Lampard, the foreman, would never even speak to a man who had a pipe in his mouth. Bill noticed a fellow member of the Society from another town, who had come in search of a job, and gave him a friendly nod. He walked on, gave in his ticket, and climbed up the outside staircase towards his workshop. There was already an atmosphere of subdued excitement, and some of the men who had stayed there for breakfast had strung up sheets of metal from the beams and were waiting with their hammers in their hand. Others were holding a hammer in one hand and a metal cylinder or an old casting in the other. Bill tied a piece of metal to a beam above his bench and picked up his hammer.

They had not been waiting long before they heard the rhythmical booming of the steam hammer and the shriller sound of the blacksmiths beating on their anvils and sheets of tin. This was followed by sounds of cheering down in the yard. Shortly afterwards, there came the hollow drum-like sound of wooden patterns being beaten with clenched fists and wooden mallets from the shop next door and more cheering. At that moment, the doors rolled open and a blushing young man slipped into the shop to the deafening sound of hammers beating on cylinders, sheets of metal and old castings. The man slipped through the smiling crowd of workmates to his bench, and the thundering peal of welcome continued for several more minutes before they all gave him three loud cheers.

They always 'rang in' any workmate when he got married. The bridegroom usually took two or three days off work after his wedding and didn't come back until 8.30 a.m. on the day of his return. After he had been 'rung in' he had to pay his 'footing' of 10s to the senior man in the shop, who also collected 'footings' from every new apprentice, from every apprentice who had 'come out of his time', and from every new man when he started work. The 'footings' ranged from 5s to a sovereign. When enough money had been collected all the men in the shop had an evening out in the pub, drinking beer, singing songs and toasting the men whose 'footings' had founded the feast. There wasn't much other relief from work, so the men always made as much of these 'ringings in' as possible.

After the excitement had died down, Bill called his apprentice over to show him how to use the files. Bill picked up a piece of metal and tested it with a straight-edged ruler. He chipped away some of the larger bumps with a chisel and then got a coarse file out of the rack and started to smooth away the bulges. When the biggest bulges had been filed away he picked up a steel plate which was completely flat, coated it with a mixture of oil and red ochre, and pressed it against the surface of the piece of metal, so that all the uneven points were coloured red. He started to remove these with a finer file. Finally he got out his scraper—a three-sided file ground to a fine point—sharpened it on his oilstone and carefully scraped away, checking his work with a ruler as he did so. When he was satisfied he tested it again with the steel plate; the whole surface came out red, showing that it was completely flat. Bill was so skilled at his work that he made it look deceptively simple. He gave John a chisel and hammer, some coarse files and a piece of metal and set him to work on it a little further down the bench where he could keep an eye on him.

Bill had liked John from the first day he came into the workshop. The lad hadn't lost his temper or sulked when he had had to go through the same ceremonies that all 'new nippers' did on their first day as an apprentice. Some of the older apprentices, who were nearly 'out of their time', had sent John over to Samuel Cousins, one of the worst-tempered 'lushingtons' in

25

the workshop, for a non-existent tool—a 'toe punch'. Samuel Cousins had obliged by giving John a kick which nearly sent him flying. Then some of the apprentices had offered to teach him how to use a hammer and chisel. One of them had jerked John's right hand so that he had hit his other hand with the hammer. But he had taken all of this in a good spirit and the other apprentices had soon accepted him as one of them. You could have a hard time if they didn't like you.

The apprentice could also have a hard life if he wasn't put in the care of a good, steady, honest workman. Some of the men exploited their apprentices greatly, using them 'to keep nix' for the foreman while they were having a sly smoke or doing 'corporation work' for themselves, which would end up as a pair of fancy, wrought-iron brackets under the shelves in their parlour. Bill never did any 'corporation work' for his own home. He thought it was far too risky to smuggle the work out of the factory under the watchful eyes of the gatekeeper. The gatekeeper had been at his job far too long to believe that a man had suddenly acquired a limp that afternoon, and usually spotted the piece of metal hidden in his trouser leg. Bill had seen the gates closed for good behind too many men who had tried that old trick.

At that moment, Bill glanced up from his work; you could always feel when something was happening in the shop. He turned round and saw Samuel Cousins slipping a coin into the hand of one of the apprentices. A few moments later the apprentice strolled casually out of the shop. Samuel Cousins was such a 'lushington' that he couldn't do without his pint at eleven o'clock, even though it was forbidden to drink or to smoke in the factory. The apprentice had to get out somehow, if he didn't want to suffer under Samuel Cousins' tongue, either by climbing over the wall or by strolling out of the factory gates as if he was on lawful business. And then he had to smuggle the beer back into the factory.

Ten minutes later he returned, his mission successfully completed. Shortly afterwards, Samuel Cousins walked out of the workshop with something bulging under his jacket. He went to the lavatory, which consisted of nothing more than a metal pole suspended over a trough of running water at the end of a dark passage. A couple of years before Mr Ashworth, the factory owner, had made a new rule that no one should use the lavatory for longer than six minutes once a day. But a deputation of three members of the Society had gone to see him—and the rule had been withdrawn.

Bill noticed a group of older apprentices talking earnestly together in a corner of the shop. A few moments later three of them went out—in the same direction as Samuel Cousins. They came back after a short interval and scattered to all sides of the shop, followed soon afterwards by Samuel Cousins, red-faced and glaring angrily at all the apprentices. No one gave him a glance, but everyone knew what had happened. The apprentices had lit a

Some Mechanics' Institutes, like this one in Bradford, were impressively large

piece of oily paper and let it float down the water towards Samuel Cousins sitting on the pole. It was an old trick, but one of the many ways the apprentices had of getting even with a craftsman they didn't like. If a man was particularly brutal towards the apprentices they'd 'smallgang' him; they'd wait up an alley for him after work, then a group of the oldest and fittest lads would attack him. There had never been a man who had come out of one of these encounters as the victor.

Bill glanced along the bench at his own apprentice. John was grinning to himself, remembering perhaps that needlessly savage kick that Samuel Cousins had given him when he had asked him for a 'toe punch'. Bill went over to look at the work John was doing, altered his grip on the file, and gave him an encouraging pat on the shoulder. He could see that John had a feeling for the metal; he felt sure that he'd qualify and become a member of the Society in seven years' time. After a few months he'd have to take John round to the Mechanics' Institute where Bill himself had studied English, mechanical drawing, applied mechanics and physics two nights a week when he had been an apprentice himself. You had to know your stuff properly, if you wanted to get anywhere in this world.

Bill took his life, his work, and his union seriously. The Amalgamated

Society of Engineers had been one of the most important factors in his life. His father had been one of the original 7,000 members of the Society when it was formed in 1851. For many years, until he had become too ill to work, his father had been the branch secretary, spending hours of his spare time keeping the accounts, writing reports for the head office in London, and attending the fortnightly branch meetings. Bill had joined the Society in his last year as an apprentice, when he was twenty years of age. He had been proposed by his father and seconded by the branch president. The entrance fee of 15s and the weekly contribution of 1s was a lot to pay, especially when you were only earning 10s a week as a final-year apprentice. But the Society provided many benefits. If you were out of work, you got a 'do' or donation from the Society of 10s a week for fourteen weeks, 7s for thirty weeks, and 6s a week from then on. If you were sick, you received 10s a week for twenty-six weeks and 5s a week after that for as long as you were ill. Although the 'do' wasn't enough for a married man to live on, you could always apply to the Society for a benevolent grant if you were really desperate. The grants came from the pockets of all the other members who were working. The grants had saved many men—and their families—from the horrors of the workhouse.

Because of these benefits it was very important to make sure that you didn't let any trash into the Society—men who might pretend that they were ill, or men who would always be out of work and living on the 'do'. Bill was always very careful to make sure that the men he introduced had steady habits and a good moral character, as the Society laid down. All the men he had recommended were still members of the Society. But some of the other 200 members of his branch didn't take such care. A number of the men they proposed had to be expelled later for not paying their weekly fees, for getting donations or sick pay under false pretences, or, occasionally, for committing a crime.

The Society had helped him to see a bit of the world before he got married and settled down. As an apprentice he had been forbidden, by the terms of his indentures, 'to play cards, dice, tables or other unlawful games', 'to haunt taverns', or 'to contract matrimony'. When he had 'come out of his time' as an apprentice, he had decided, like many other engineers, to try his luck in London. The wages were 4s or 5s a week higher than they were in other parts of the country and he wanted to acquire the 'London polish' from the engineers in the capital, who were generally thought to be the most skilled in the United Kingdom.

His father encouraged him in the idea. Bill had been earning a man's rate of pay for only a few months when his chance came. The firm was short of orders and some men had to be sacked. Although Mr Ashworth would have kept him on Bill volunteered to go, to save the job of a married member of

This Indenture made the seventeenth day of September One thousand eight hundred and seventy two **Between** Henry Selby Hele Shaw a minor of the age of Eighteen years or thereabouts of the first part Henry Shaw of London Street Paddington in the county of Middlesex Gentleman (the Father of the said Henry Selby Hele Shaw) of the second part Edwin Rouch of the Mardy Ke Iron Works in the City of Bristol Engineer of the third part and William Robert Howard Leaker of the Iron Works aforesaid Engineer the Copartner in Business with the said Edwin Rouch of the fourth part **Witnesseth** that the said Henry Selby Hele Shaw of his own free will and accord and with the consent and approbation of the said Father (testified by their respective execution of these presents) **Doth** hereby put place and bind himself Apprentice to the said Edwin Rouch to learn his said trade or business of a Millwright and Mechanical Engineer in all its branches and with him after the manner of an Apprentice to serve from the twenty ninth day of July last for and during the term of Three years from thence next following and to be fully complete and ended during which term the said Apprentice his said Master faithfully shall and will serve his secrets keep and lawful commands gladly obey and perform He shall do no damage to his said Master nor see any done by others but to the utmost of his power shall prevent or forthwith give notice to his said Master of the same The Goods of his said Master he shall not waste nor lend them unlawfully to any Hurt to his said Master he shall not do cause or procure to be done Taverns Inns or Alehouses he shall not frequent At Cards Dice Tables or any other unlawful Games he shall not play From the service of his said Master without his previous consent

Part of the four-page indenture of an engineering apprentice of 1872

the Society. By that time he had bought some clothes and saved two or three pounds. He asked his father, as the branch secretary, to give him a travelling card, so that he could draw his 'do' from a branch in London. With his few possessions, he travelled down to London by train. On his arrival he went to see the branch secretary, who arranged for him to stay at the pub where the Society held its fortnightly meetings. Because he was young it didn't take him long to find a job, though the first factory was a real 'slaughterhouse' where the men had to work very hard and the discipline was strict. After a month he went to another factory where the conditions were better.

He got good, cheap lodgings with one of the married men who worked in the factory, and 'found for himself' except at the week-ends when he had his meals with the family. The wife was a nice, homely woman. He called her 'mother' while she called him Bill, and did little jobs for him and gave him extra meals for which she wouldn't take a penny.

Bill really enjoyed his two years in London, when he always seemed to have plenty of money to spend. You could do just what you liked down there; no one knew and no one cared. He had his hair cut short, which was the fashionable style among young mechanics then, bought himself two sporty-looking suits, some fancy caps and some red-and-white mufflers. On Saturday nights, he and four or five of his mates would hire a smart trap to take them to a 6d 'hop' in a dancing academy or a saloon near the pleasure park at Greenwich. Or, sometimes, they'd have a 1s 6d dinner there instead. Other nights they'd have a few drinks and end up at the local Theatre Royal clutching their bags or oranges and nuts. His favourite plays were *The Convict's Return* and *The Negro of Wapping*.

On Sunday morning he'd get up late. About ten o'clock, his landlady would bring up his breakfast of some special 'relish' that he liked, such as herrings or sausages. Then he'd have a wash, take out his 'Sunday best', which he kept in a clothes box under the bed, and go off to the barber's for a shave. The barber's shop was always packed on Sunday mornings, with the barber and two or three assistant shavers hard at work from 10 a.m. to 3 p.m. While you waited, you could have a 'glass of medicine'—spiced rum, gin or whisky—if you were known to the barber and were willing to pay 4d instead of 1d for a shave.

In the summer afternoons, he'd often take a trip on a steamer from London Bridge to Greenwich Park, with its exciting crowds of foreigners and English people of all kinds and classes, its stalls and its Indians selling sweet-meats from trays suspended by a cord around their neck. If he was lucky, he'd have a girl on his arm—a milliner, a dressmaker, or a 'lady's maid'—dressed up 'to kill' in her smartest frock and Parisian kid gloves. He'd buy himself some Havana cigars—at seven for 1s—and treat her to a 9d meal of tea and shrimps before they returned on the evening steamer.

Melodramas, preferably with live horses and real coaches on the stage, were one of the favourite forms of entertainment of the Victorian working classes

An artist's impression of Sunday morning in the cramped home of a London workman in the 1870s

Crowded paddle steamers set out from Westminster for a pleasure trip along the Thames

It was on one of these trips down-river to Gravesend that he noticed a woman sitting on a bench in the docks, with some shining new cooking tins among her scanty luggage, waiting to board a ship which was going to take her abroad. It made him think of emigrating himself. The Society had branches in many different parts of the world, in India, Malta, Australia, Canada, and the first one had just been opened in the United States—at Buffalo in New York State. Bill made a few inquiries from the branch secretary. He found that it was easy for a man with the Society's card to get a job anywhere. Some of the foreign branches would even help you with the fare. Conditions were much better overseas; the wages were higher and the hours were often shorter. The engineers in Melbourne, Australia, were just on the verge of getting an eight-hour day, while most British engineers, except for those in London and Manchester, were still working a ten-hour day six days a week. Even now they still had a nine-hour day.

But when he weighed it all up he decided not to go. He'd been away from home for two years and was beginning to miss his family, his friends and his home town. Furthermore, he'd just heard that his father wasn't too well. So he went back to Loomtown again. Less than two years later he married Sally Ratcliffe, who worked as a weaver in a local mill.

At that moment, the bell rang again. It was one o'clock, time for dinner. They had an hour, so Bill could afford to walk home at a more leisurely pace. Some of the younger men in lodgings or those who lived a long way from their work went to a nearby cooking depot for their meal. There hadn't been such places when Bill had been working as a young man in London. He'd been there once or twice himself when his wife wasn't feeling well. The dining room was rather barely furnished and no smoking or drinking was allowed, but you were served by waitresses and the food was cheap and well cooked. You could have a bowl of soup, bread and cheese, and a cup of tea or coffee for 3d, or a plate of meat and potatoes for the same price. A glass of milk or some bread cost $\frac{1}{2}$d.

When he arrived home his children were already waiting. After a quick wash in the scullery, he sat down at the table too. His wife gave him the largest share of the slices of warmed-up mutton, cabbage and potatoes, and then he ate the one remaining piece of cheese. He felt warm and comfortable sitting at the table beside the blazing fire, but it didn't seem very long before it was time for him to return to the factory again.

Back at his bench, Bill settled down to his work once more. The afternoons weren't so bad now, since they'd won a nine-hour day in the previous year. They finished work at 5 p.m. instead of 6 p.m. It also meant that they finished work at 1 p.m. on Saturday, which was the easiest day of all. Work really stopped at 12.30 p.m., as they were usually allowed half an hour to tidy up their benches and to put their tools in order for the following week, while the labourers swept the floors. They owed their shorter hours to the Society men in Newcastle, who had won their strike for a nine-hour day in 1871, even though the employers had tried to break it by importing foreign workers from Germany and Belgium. After that, most of the employers in other parts of the country had conceded a nine-hour day—without a strike.

There was quite a cheerful atmosphere in the workshop that afternoon, as they were paid on Friday—another change that had been made in the last year. Everyone was waiting for the two labourers to carry in a table and set it up in a corner of the shop. At that moment, there was a disturbingly loud creaking noise from the ceiling and everyone looked up anxiously at the shafting above, which was running hot. There were loud shouts of 'Oil! Oil!' and 'Strappie!' and almost immediately 'Strappie' Marshall came dashing in with a ladder and a can and climbed up among the straps and pulleys to oil the shafts. There was a risk of fire, or of the shafts breaking, if he didn't oil them quickly enough.

About two hours later the table was put up and shortly afterwards the foreman, carrying the money bags, and the cashier, clutching a large leather-bound ledger, came in. The men filed past the table—the craftsmen first, then the labourers and finally the apprentices. Bill received a gold sovereign and some other coins—36s 6d in all. His basic rate of pay was 32s a week, but he had worked overtime until eight o'clock on two nights, which was paid at time and a quarter. In the best weeks he could make £2, when he did plenty of overtime and was paid 'walking money' for being sent to repair an engine some distance from the shop and 'dirty money' for the extra wear and tear on his clothes that repairs entailed. Most of the skilled men got about the same basic wage. The labourers earned about £1 a week and the apprentices started at 2s 6d or 3s which rose to 10s or more a week in their final year.

Bill walked back to his bench for the last hour. Just as he was thinking that it must be nearly time for the bell, one of his mates came hurrying over with his hand over his left eye. Bill quickly dipped his hands in the cask of water beneath the bench and roughly dried them. Taking his mate over to the window, he rolled up his top eyelid and with his knife flicked away the speck of grit in his eye. It often happened when someone was working at the grinding wheel. You needed a steady hand and some skill to get the grit out so expertly. It was the only 'medical' attention that any of them ever received at work.

The final bell rang. Bill put on his jacket and cap, and with his shop jacket rolled up under his arm, left the shop. He hurried home, knowing that his wife would be waiting for his wages to buy their food for tea.

3. AT SCHOOL

Earlier that day, after their breakfast of porridge and bread and butter, George and Sarah set off for school. Sarah was wearing a frock, a clean pinafore, white socks and black shoes, while George was dressed in the little grey tweed suit that he always wore to school. Before they left, Mrs Boddington gave George his weekly school fees of 2d wrapped up in a piece of paper. She was just going to wrap Sarah's fees of 4d in a clean handkerchief when she noticed some crumbs of bread and porridge on George's chin. Spitting on the handkerchief, she wiped his chin; she always liked to see them going off clean and respectable-looking to school.

After warning George not to play with any rough boys or to get into any fights, Mrs Boddington stood on the front doorstep watching them walk side by side towards the exit from the court. A few doors further down, a neatly dressed little girl with a clean face and her hair in ringlets came running out of her house to join them. She was the only child in the court that Mrs Boddington would let her own children play with: the others were much too rough and dirty. All the other families were much larger than her own. There was a cabman who had ten children, a labourer who had eight, and two couples who had six. Mrs Boddington continued to watch the children until they reached the archway which led into the street, and then went back into the house to do her work.

When the three children reached the street, they parted company. George turned left towards the new Board school, which he had been attending for the last few months. The two little girls went the other way, towards the dame's school, where George had also been a pupil from the age of four to five. Mrs Boddington visited a number of dame's schools before she had made her choice. Some of these 'adventure' schools, as they were called, were totally unsuitable.

She visited one which was held in the kitchen of a little house like her own, with only three old desks and not enough forms for all the children to sit on so that some of them had to squat on the bare floor. If there were too many children, some were sent upstairs to play by themselves. Everything looked dirty, including the old woman who ran the school. When Mrs Boddington went in, the 'dame' was sitting in the middle of a circle of girls who were knitting, while two older girls were trying to keep a group of younger children quiet in a corner of the room. For the privilege of sending her children to this school, so Mrs Boddington was informed, she would have to pay 6d a week, which was as much as some of the best Church schools charged. After visiting another 'adventure' school which was equally unsatisfactory, Mrs Boddington had found a suitable school in a street nearby. It was run by Mrs Perkins, the widow of a clerk who had worked in one of the local mills.

Sarah and her friend arrived at Mrs Perkins' house, which was slightly larger than the ones they lived in. They opened the front door and went into the kitchen which had been fitted out as a schoolroom. The room was clean and there was a good fire blazing in the grate. The walls had been recently whitewashed, and were decorated with a few red-and-yellow cards, showing some of the letters of the alphabet, and some coloured prints of Biblical subjects, including Moses leading his people to the promised land. A row of desks and forms extended along the two longer walls and Mrs Perkins sat by the shorter wall, facing the fireplace. She was a plump, good-natured woman of about fifty. She always wore a well-fitting, black dress with a little, frilly, white collar and a small, trimmed cap perched on her grey hair.

A Victorian elementary school. Some are still in use a century later

There were about twenty boys and girls in the school, ranging in age from three to six.

Sarah and her friend sat down in their places at the end of a form nearest to the schoolmistress. The forms soon filled up, with the oldest children sitting furthest away from Mrs Perkins. All the children were clean and neatly dressed; practically all of them were the sons and daughters of skilled workers and shopkeepers.

The morning started, as it always did, with prayers and a hymn. Then Mrs Perkins told them to fold their arms and to sit upright while she read them a story about Moses. Afterwards she gave the older children some sums to do on their slates, and then gathered the younger ones around her to teach them the ABC. She held up coloured cards in turn, each one printed with a different letter of the alphabet, while the children chanted the verse they had learnt for each. They started:

> A is an angel, who in heaven does dwell,
> B stands for Bethlehem, as the scriptures tell . . .

Then Mrs Perkins would hold up a card and ask one of the children what the letter was. They all tried hard, for if they made more than three mistakes Mrs Perkins would make them stand in the middle of the group and put the dunce's cap with its attached donkey's ears on their head, while all the other children jeered:

> Dunce, dunce, double D
> Can't say your ABC.

At 11 a.m. they had a break for play, either in the small backyard, which also contained the privy, or in the street outside. For the rest of the morning the older children copied words on to their slates, while Mrs Perkins told the younger ones a story. They went home for dinner from 12.30 to 2 p.m.

The afternoon always started in a brisk way, so that the children would not fall asleep after their midday meal. When all the children were seated, Mrs Perkins called out 'Attention!' in a loud, commanding way. The children sat upright with their arms extended straight in front of them. 'Down!' Mrs Perkins called, and they let their arms fall to the sides of their body. Then, led by Mrs Perkins, they all started to clap their hands vigorously together while they chanted:

> Clap, clap, clap away,
> This is the way to exercise,
> As teacher says we may.

From time to time, at Mrs Perkins' command, they shot out their arms or clapped their hands above their heads, while the forms rocked and shook beneath their jerking bodies. This always went on for over half an hour, by which time they were all as warm as toast, and ready for another break in the yard or in the street outside. The last period of the day was taken up by sewing for the older girls, arithmetic for the older boys, and more practice of the ABC or simple words, such as 'pit, pat, pet' for the younger children.

Meanwhile, George had been undergoing much the same sort of treatment at his Board school. The schoolroom was large and draughty with a raised platform at one end for the masters. The children sat at wooden desks on three sides of a square, with space enough for forty pupils in each row. To look after them there were a teacher and two pupil-teachers, young girls of fourteen who were being trained by the headmaster in his spare time.

The morning was taken up by writing on slates, reading and arithmetic, and in the afternoon there was needlework and sewing for the girls and sums for the boys. The lessons George liked most were playing with the sets of wooden bricks, which they did once a week, and singing, which they always had immediately after the dinner break. That afternoon they learnt a new song:

> I must not throw upon the floor
> The crust I cannot eat;
> For many little hungry ones
> Would think it quite a treat.
>
> My parents labour very hard
> To get me wholesome food;
> Then I must never waste a bit
> That would do others good
>
> For wilful waste makes woeful want
> And I may live to say,
> 'Oh! how I wish I had the bread
> That once I threw away.'

The song was accompanied by gestures which they had practised with the teacher beforehand.

Although George liked the song, it wasn't a particularly suitable choice for many members of his class. Every day, more and more dirty, diseased and hungry children were admitted to the school, as the new attendance officers visited the poorer houses in the district and threatened the parents with prosecution if they didn't send their children to school. The new children

LESSON 8.

ad	ed	id	od	ud
bad	bed	bid	cod	bud
had	fed	did	hod	cud
lad	Ned	hil	nod	mud
mad	red	kid	rod	sud
pad	Ted	lid	sod	
sad	wed	rid		

He is a bad lad. Did the mad lad rub the cat? No, but he led the ox to the wet hut. She is to wed Pat. He hid the cat in the vat. The fat kid got in the mud. Ned fed the ox. He got a cod, but he did not get a kid or a cat. She put the bud in the hut, not on the bed. It is a red ox, but not a fat ox. The lid of the pot is in the hut, is it not? Do not rob the cat, but let her get the rat. It is so fat. Ted is a lad, and he had a cod in the mud. Go to bed, as it is bad not to do so.

It was from books such as these that children learnt to read a hundred years ago

used to spit on the floor and wipe their inky hands on their ragged clothes. Their noses were always running and many of them had scabs and sores. One or two had no boots or shoes. George was frightened of them. If he ever brought a bun or a crust of bread to school, they tried to snatch it from him. He had been much happier at Mrs Perkins' school.

Just before school finished at 4 p.m., all the children were given a handbill with strict instructions to give it to their parents. George gave it to his mother when he reached home. Mrs Boddington took the handbill over to the window, as her eyesight wasn't very good, and read it slowly to herself. The handbill was headed: LOOMTOWN SCHOOL BOARD. It reminded parents that it was compulsory for all children to attend school from the age of five to thirteen. Only children who were over ten years of age and had passed the Standard Four examination could be exempted, and allowed to work half-time in the mills or factories. It also pointed out that if children stayed away from school, without excuse, their parents could be taken before the magistrates and fined 2s 6d.

Mrs Boddington put the handbill on the mantelpiece to show it to her husband when he came home. She picked up the kettle and was just going into the scullery to fill it when she noticed that George was scratching himself again. She sighed to herself. He must have caught another flea from those dirty children at school.

She was sorry now that she had ever sent him there at all. But when she had heard that a new Board school was being built in the district, both she and her husband had been extremely pleased. It had been opened that year by the chairman of the School Board—the first of the eight new Board schools to be completed. It was a huge building, almost as impressive in its own way, as the new parish church which had been opened two years before. The school was built of brick and stone, and was surmounted by a large bell tower, which also acted as a ventilation shaft. It could accommodate 800 children, and was divided into three sections for boys, girls, and infants from five to seven. There were three separate playgrounds, two of them shut off from the street by tall, spiked railings, and the third on the flat roof.

Mrs Boddington had been among the first of the parents to enrol her child when the school year had started in the second week of August. Holding George by the hand, she had been taken by a teacher into a corridor where she waited to see the headmaster. She had been as impressed by him as she was by the appearance of the school. He was a refined, well-spoken man, who had explained with great enthusiasm all the benefits that the school could provide. The infants' school would give instruction in reading, writing and arithmetic and special attention would also be paid to singing. In the boys' school, there would also be lessons in English grammar, geography, history, drawing, music and drill—for which a drill sergeant had been specially engaged. The fees started at 2d a week, rising to 5d for the eldest pupils. There was a fortnight's holiday at Christmas and in the summer and

Crowded benches in an infants' 'gallery' class

a week at Whitsun, with Easter Monday and the afternoon of Shrove Tuesday also free.

Mrs Boddington had been greatly impressed and had enrolled her son at once. She had not realized that so many rough, dirty children would be forced into the school. Fortunately, George wouldn't have to mix with them much longer, as they were moving to a new house in a better district soon. When they moved, she'd send him to a nice Church school, even if the fees were higher. You got what you paid for in this world, she thought, as she went into the scullery to fill the kettle.

4. AT HOME

Mrs Boddington's day started at 7 a.m. She was a thinnish, little woman whose hair was already turning grey, even though she was only thirty. Her hands were rough and hardened by continual scrubbing and cleaning, and her nails were cracked and broken. Deep down in the pores of her lined face there was grit and grime which she could never scrub out. But she looked cheerful and was often smiling.

When she got up, she put on her frock and an apron, which was always crisp and clean at the beginning of the day but soiled and dirty by the end. She wore a little mobcap on her head.

Her first task of the day, winter and summer, was to light a fire in the kitchen range, as she had no other means of cooking. Kneeling down by the grate, she broke up the clinker with a poker and picked out the pieces she could re-use once the fire was burning. Then she swept the flue and carried the soot and ash out to the tub in the street, where Bill had left it to be collected. She lit the fire with a few dry sticks from the bundles of wood she bought from a barrow man who also sold powdered white clay for cleaning the doorstep. He was one of the many pedlars who came round to the court. Another regular caller was a gipsy woman who sold wooden spoons. And at the week-ends in particular the streets resounded with the cries of women and children selling all kinds of tasty foods:

'Fine bloaters, fine fresh bloaters! Prime smoked haddock!'
'Fine fresh shrimps, penny a pint! Shrimp, Oh!'
'Watercresses, all fresh-gathered watercresses! Two bundles for a
    ha'penny!'

When the fire was burning she went into the scullery and washed her hands under the tap. There was no sink, only a slopstone—a flat stone slab with a hole at one end for the water to drain away. As the pipe led directly into the sewer, without any trap, there was often a terrible smell from the drain, which Mrs Boddington always blamed for any illness in the family.

She got her two children up, made them have a wash in the tin bowl in the scullery, and saw that they were neatly dressed for school. While they were doing this she laid the table with a few bowls, plates and mugs, and some knives and spoons. On the kitchen range she heated up the saucepan of porridge that she had made the previous day, stirring it with a wooden spoon so that it did not burn. She was just cutting the bread and buttering it thinly when her husband returned for breakfast. She served him first because he had so little time.

As soon as her husband had gone back to work and she had seen her two children off to school, work really started in earnest. She didn't know how some of the other women in the court with six or more children managed, though it was obvious by the appearance of their children and their dirty, front doorsteps that they weren't very successful at doing so. Filling a bucket with water, she carried it out to the front door, and on her hands and knees started to scrub the doorstep. She did this every morning except on Sunday, when she didn't want to be seen working. So she always scrubbed the step twice on Saturday, once in the morning and again late at night. In spite of all her efforts the step was always black with soot and grime again by the next day. Sometimes her whole life seemed to be an unending, and losing, battle against those two enemies—soot and grit—which infiltrated everywhere, into your home, into your clothes, even into the pores of your skin. When she had scrubbed the step thoroughly, she scattered a little white powdered clay on it and scrubbed it in. Afterwards she blackleaded the knocker.

Now that her house looked clean and respectable from the outside she turned her attention to the interior. The house was not very large. There were two narrow bedrooms upstairs, which were only 6 feet high; a kitchen about 13 feet long and 12 feet wide and a slightly smaller scullery downstairs; and a cellar for storing coal. They cooked and ate in the kitchen and washed in the scullery, which also had a brick-built copper, heated by a coal fire. In this she heated water for the weekly bath for the children and herself, which they took in a tin bath in front of the kitchen range.

The rooms were simply and barely furnished. Only in the kitchen had some attempt been made to provide a little comfort or luxury. There was a rag rug by the hearth and several cheap china ornaments on the shelf above the kitchen range. Hanging on the whitewashed walls there were one or two cheap coloured prints, which her husband had framed. Her most prized possession was a small inlaid table, which her husband had made for their fifth wedding anniversary. He had also fitted some shelves into the recess by the range. In addition, there was a plain, square table, five chairs, a mirror and her workbox, in which she kept her sewing materials.

Although the house was so small and so sparsely furnished, Mrs Boddington felt sure that she would never have got through all her work unless she had had a regular plan for every day of the week. On Monday, she brushed all the Sunday clothes and put them away carefully in the clothes boxes under

43

the bed, where they were stored until the following week. On Tuesday, she did her washing at the public baths and wash-house, where her husband also went on Saturday for his weekly bath. The wash-house was situated on the ground floor of the public baths. It was well equipped, with fifteen separate stands, each with its own tub for washing clothes and another zinc-lined tub for boiling. There were three mangles, a machine for extracting water from the clothes, and a large drying room which was so hot that the clothes could be taken out dry in five minutes. Although it cost 3d for two hours, Mrs Boddington thought it was money well spent. You didn't have to drape all your clothes over the furniture in the kitchen to dry them, as you did if you washed them in the copper in the scullery. And she certainly wasn't going to dry her clothes out in the street, as some of the other women in the court did. Not only was it common, but the clothes soon got covered with soot and grime so that they became almost as dirty as they had been before you washed them. On Wednesday she did her ironing with a flat iron heated on the kitchen range. On Thursday she swept and thoroughly cleaned the bedrooms, and on Friday she cleaned the downstairs rooms.

Saturday was one of the busiest days of the week, as she always tried to have the whole house spotlessly clean before her husband came home just after one o'clock. She got up early on Saturday so that she could blacklead the kitchen range and polish the fire irons until they were gleaming. Then she scrubbed the doorstep, cleaned and tidied up and cooked the dinner, so that it was ready by the time her husband came home.

Immediately after dinner she started shopping, which always took most of the afternoon. The grocer kept most of his goods—tea, coffee, sugar, pepper, dried peas, oatmeal, flour, pepper—in large wooden drawers or casks behind the wooden counter. For every purchase, the grocer or his assistant had to twist a paper bag out of a piece of paper, fill it up and weigh it on the scales. Butter had to be sliced off with wooden butter pats from the huge block on the counter, weighed, patted into shape and re-weighed.

Recently she'd changed her grocer. The previous one had talked her into buying a special blend of tea by promising to give her a coloured German print if she bought 2 lb., an ornament for the mantelpiece if she bought 4 lb., and a pair of glass candlesticks if she bought 6 lb. Although the tea was cheap—only 2s 6d a pound—it was rubbishy stuff which never made a decent cup. After she'd bought enough to get her German print she'd gone to another grocer.

She bought her vegetables in a street market, often late at night when the prices were reduced, and her milk and eggs from the town dairy, where the cows were kept in stalls at the back of the shop. The milk was ladled straight out of the churn into your jug. Then George and Sarah always wanted to spend their week's pocket money, even though they'd only been given it that

Washing day contrasts! Clothes lines in a London slum and the new baths at Barrow-in-Furness, which also contained a laundry room. The working men's institute is a little further down the road (on the left of the picture)

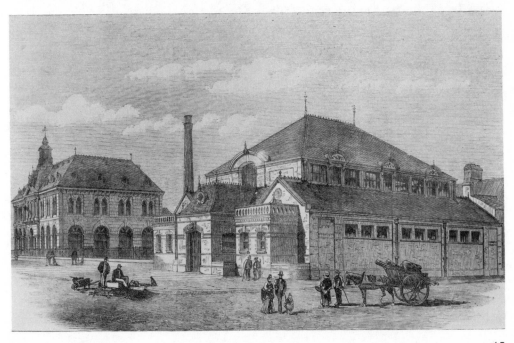

morning. She took them to a little sweet shop in an underground kitchen, where an old man and woman made the sweets in vats and pans on an old range at the back of the shop. Her children would take ages deciding how they would spend their penny, whether they should spend it all on five bars of toffee, or whether they should buy only two bars for $\frac{1}{2}$d and $\frac{1}{2}$ oz. of rum almonds, or amber jujubes or a piece of peppermint rock as well. In the evening they always had some 'relish' such as black pudding, faggots, or a pie and peas from the pie shop round the corner, and as a weekly treat George and Sarah would be allowed to stay up late to share the hot evening meal. After they were in bed, Mrs Boddington would usually go out shopping again to buy the meat for the Sunday dinner, or some material for clothes, or a new shawl for herself. The shops did not close until 11 p.m. or midnight on Saturdays. And she also had to scrub her front doorstep again, and if she had the energy and the time, to bake a pie or a tart for Sunday dinner.

In addition to all these carefully planned weekly tasks, there were many other jobs for her to do each day—the cooking, making beds, and tidying. She always liked to have her work done by the time her husband came home at 5 p.m. She usually made, mended, and darned clothes in the evening.

As it was Friday, she started work on the downstairs rooms. When she had swept them out thoroughly, scrubbed the scullery floor, tidied up and dusted, it was time to think about getting the dinner. She rarely did any shopping on Friday morning, as by then she usually never had a penny left, apart from the 6d for the school fees. She always had to plan her meals so that she would have something left over to make a decent dinner on Friday. That day they were having warmed-up slices of mutton, boiled potatoes and cabbage. There was enough cheese left for her husband to have bread and cheese afterwards. She peeled the potatoes, prepared the cabbage, and put them in saucepans to boil on the kitchen range. Once they were boiling, she moved them further away from the fire, until they were just simmering. At half-past twelve, just before Sarah returned, she put the slices of cold mutton at the bottom of the oven, where it was coolest, so that they would get warm but not shrivel up. She was just laying the table when Sarah came in, followed about ten minutes later by George. Mrs Boddington asked them what had happened at school, and made them wash their hands and faces before she would allow them to sit at the table. They were all ready and waiting when the door opened shortly after one o'clock and her husband came in for dinner.

5. AFTERNOON

By two o'clock Mrs Boddington was alone again with only the washing up to be done. On Friday afternoons she usually had a chance to put her feet up, but she rarely did so. She always liked to be on the go. That was what had made it so hard for her earlier in the year when she'd had a baby prematurely; it had been born dead at seven months. For weeks afterwards she'd felt ill and out of sorts with no energy to do anything. She'd lost another baby two years before that. In her heart she couldn't say she was really sorry that she still had only two children instead of four. It was all right for the rich to have large families, but for the likes of them, it could only drag you down into the gutter.

Bill's father had also died earlier in the year at the age of fifty-six. But he couldn't grumble, as he'd had a good long life; many men were dead long before they reached forty. And in one way it had been a merciful release, as he'd been ill for the whole two years that he'd been living with them.

In some ways, then, it had been a hard year, but there were always others who were worse off. At least she didn't have to go charring for twelve hours a day for 2s 6d, or work in the mills, as some of the other women in the court did. Mrs Boddington, like most of the local girls, had started work as a 'piecer' in a local mill at the age of ten, assisting a spinner who had made her really earn the few shillings he paid her every week. It was so hot in the mill that he wore only a thin shirt with the sleeves rolled up, white cotton drawers which came down to his ankles, and nothing on his feet. He was always in a hurry because he was paid for how much he produced. She and another 'piecer' had to watch the threads on the spindles and join them together again if they broke. But what really frightened her was when he made her dash in among the whirling wheels of the machine to clean away the cotton fluff while the machine was still in motion.

When she was older she'd transferred to the weaving shed, where she was put in charge of four power looms. It was just as hot in there and even moister, so that some of the girls wore short skirts. Mrs Boddington thought it was quite disgraceful for them to show their legs like that. She wore an apron and a skirt and a band round her hair so that it wouldn't get caught in the machinery. The noise was so deafening that they couldn't talk to each other and had to communicate by signs. She had always hated working in the mill. At least she didn't have to suffer that for sixty hours a week any more, though she spent just as many hours every week, or even more, looking after her own home.

But everything was going to be much better for all of them soon. Sometimes she still couldn't believe that they were going to move into a house of their own. It would have been impossible for her parents to buy a house, and even now there weren't many families who could afford to do so. She thought she'd just go to see how the builders were getting on—as she did almost every week. Slipping on her black shawl, she went out and turned away from the centre of the town. The new house was further out, but that wouldn't bother her as she rarely went to the town centre. Her life was bounded by the small shops and street markets around the narrow courts and alleys of her neighbourhood. She wouldn't have wanted to live in the centre of the town, where everything always seemed to be in a process of constant change. Whenever she visited it, there seemed to be some new building: a new church, a new hospital, a new railway station, a new wholesale market, a new shop, or a new refreshment and luncheon bar, with dining and billiard saloons, and a private entrance for ladies in a side street. But none of these places had any connection with her own life; it could have been some foreign country, as far as she was concerned.

It had been a hard struggle for them to save 2s 6d a week with the Loomtown Building Society for the past six years. They had started saving almost immediately they were married. Every week, even if you were ill or unemployed, you had to find the 2s 6d unless you wanted to be fined. And all the time you still had to go on paying your 4s rent for the house you lived in. But the long struggle had been worthwhile. With the interest on the money they had saved, they had enough to put down a deposit of £40 on the house —one-fifth of the total price—and still have a few pounds to spare. They were going to borrow the rest of the money from the building society and pay it back at 4s 6d a week. In thirteen years the house would be theirs. Everything had been arranged by a group of six gentlemen who had formed a Society for Improved Dwellings in Loomtown. They had bought the land, and found an architect and a solicitor who did all the work at a smaller fee than they normally charged.

She walked along the streets, which were almost as bleak, and just as bare of trees, as those she lived in, until she came to the site where the row of twelve houses were being built. They were really handsome, Mrs Boddington thought, with their steep, sloping roofs of slate, their new red bricks, and their black-and-white brick arches above the windows and doors. Each house had its own small front garden, and a backyard where a water closet was situated. She'd never seen one until she'd been shown around the house when it was being built. Upstairs there was a large bedroom which was as big as the two in her present house put together, with a closet for hanging up the clothes. There was also another smaller bedroom on that floor. Downstairs there was a parlour, a good-sized kitchen and, jutting out into the backyard, a scullery with a sink, a cupboard for pots and pans and a copper boiler. In the basement there was a pantry with a stone table and a small cellar for storing coal and firewood. There was even gas lighting in the downstairs rooms, though she didn't know how she'd get on with that.

In her own mind she'd already decided how she would furnish some of the rooms. She'd make some nice heavy curtains to hang at the two windows in the parlour. And she'd buy a few more ornaments to put on the mantelpiece above the open fireplace. Later on she hoped to buy a sofa, and perhaps an armchair. She'd dust the parlour every day, but never use it except on Sundays.

Life would be so much better for all of them. She'd already seen one or two of the older women who would be her neighbours. They seemed to be more like her, so that it would be easier to have a gossip if she had a moment to spare. In the court where she lived she kept herself to herself; there was only one other woman she ever spoke to. She'd already found a nice Church school for George in the neighbourhood, and as they took children from the age of three, Sarah would also be able to go there. The new house was too far away from the factory for her husband to come home for breakfast. But she'd already decided that somehow she'd find the $4\frac{1}{2}$d for breakfast every day, so that Bill could go to that coffee shop opposite the factory gates where the foreman also went. It shouldn't be too difficult, as they'd be better off when they moved. They were spending 6s 6d a week on rent and building society payments now; but when they moved they'd be paying only 4s 6d a week to the building society. Even after they'd paid the rates they'd still be better off.

She stood on the pavement for several minutes, watching the builders at work on the roof. They had nearly finished it now; it wouldn't be many more weeks before they could move in. She walked slowly back to the court. Outside in the street there was a covered van and an open dustcart, drawn by horses. As she entered the court, three men wearing huge 'fan-tail' hats which covered the back of their necks, and shirts hanging outside their trousers, came out of the court. They were carrying the wooden pails from the privies, which were exchanged for empty ones every week. The ashtub had been emptied already, so she carried it inside. At that moment Sarah returned from school. Mrs Boddington told her that the builders had nearly finished their new house and that they would be able to move into it soon. Shortly afterwards George came back from school. The children were both hungry so she cut them each a slice of bread, which was all she could give them until Bill came home with the wages.

It wasn't long before he arrived. While he was washing his hands in the scullery she poured him out a cup of tea. He came back into the kitchen and put his wages down on the table. Bill was a good husband, she thought, not like some men who gave their wives only part of their wages. Many wives did not even know what their husbands earned.

Mrs Boddington counted out the money on the kitchen table. With his overtime he'd had another good week, and she thought they could afford a little 'relish' for their tea. She sent the children off to buy four bloaters and to get ½ lb. of butter and 1 oz. of German yeast. She counted out 5s and gave it to her husband. Out of this he had to pay his union 1s a week and his friendly society 2s a month. He also had to pay 2d a week for his bath on Saturday afternoon at the public baths, and to buy any materials and tools he needed for making furniture for the home and for repairing his family's boots and shoes. He also paid for any trips they made to the parks or to the seaside. The few shillings that remained went on tobacco, which cost 2d an ounce, and beer, which cost 2d a pint.

Mrs Boddington always felt wealthy on Friday night with over 30s in her hand, but the money didn't go far once you'd paid your regular expenses. Every week she had to spend at least 23s 6d on essentials:

	s	d
Bread, five 4 lb. loaves	2	8½
Flour, 8 lb., for making bread and pies	1	4
Meat, 4 lb.	3	0
Liver, ½ lb.		2
Butter, 1 lb.	1	4
Lard, 1 lb.		10
Cheese, 1 lb.		7
Sugar, 2 lb.	1	0
Tea, ½ lb.	1	9
Milk, 8 pints	1	0
Eggs		4½
Potatoes and vegetables	1	0
Coal, oil, candles	1	0
Rent	4	0
Building society	2	6
Wash-house		3
School fees		6
Pocket money		2

When she had given Bill his 5s it left only 3s 6d a week out of his basic wage for everything else. There were many other foodstuffs she had to buy from time to time: oatmeal at 2d a pound; treacle at 3d; split peas at 2d; Goodall's baking powder at 1d a packet. Most of the 'relishes' they had at the week-end—bacon, stewed eels, whelks, shrimps, bloaters—were quite expensive. Then there was all the soap and cleaning materials, and the clothes and materials for dressmaking to buy, and the crockery to replace when it was broken. If any of them were ever ill she always tried a patent medicine before she called in a doctor. Holloway's ointment was good for stiff joints, skin diseases and old sores, while Ede's patent American blood-purifying pills could be tried if you were suffering from bronchitis, sciatica or rheumatism. There were many other similar medicines, but they were all expensive; Ede's pills cost 1s 1½d a box. But it was still cheaper than a visit to the doctor. Every week it was always a great struggle to make ends meet, but she always managed somehow, even when Bill did no overtime.

6. EVENING

Just before they had their meal of bloaters, bread and butter, and tea, Mrs Boddington lit the two oil lamps in the kitchen. When they had finished eating she asked her husband to fetch her a bucket of coal from the cellar. She wanted to do some baking that evening. While Bill was fetching the coal she got out a bowl and mixed some flour, salt and German yeast together, and put the dough in a bowl covered with a cloth by the kitchen fire.

When Bill returned he took one of the oil lamps out into the scullery to have a wash and a shave. Afterwards he went upstairs to put on his second-best clothes: cord trousers, a jacket and waistcoat, a sporty cap and a bright-coloured muffler. Normally he didn't wear them until Saturday afternoon, but he was going to the fortnightly meeting of his friendly society, the Order of Oddfellows, and as he had a special duty to perform there he wanted to look his best. He came downstairs, stood in front of the mirror in the kitchen and set his cap at a jaunty angle. After saying goodbye to his wife and children he went out, jingling the coins in his pocket.

There was always a cheerful, busy atmosphere in the streets on Friday nights. Women thronged the small gas-lit shops and the street markets, lit by flaring paraffin lamps, to buy the goods they had been deprived of for the previous two days. Groups of older apprentices and young men who had just 'come out of their time' prowled the streets in pairs and groups in search of amusement. Not everyone was bent on pleasure. Silhouetted on the blinds of many windows were the shadows of women crouched over their needle-work or hatmaking, at which they laboured far into the night for a few shillings a week.

The town contained many different kinds of drinking places. There were the huge, gaudily decorated gin palaces, where old red-eyed men and women could be seen staring gloomily into their 2d glasses of 'Old Tom'. There were riotous 'singing saloons', where the night's jokes and laughter usually ended in drunken fights and brawls. There were dingy little beerhouses, where ragged men and women escaped from the even greater squalor of their own cellar homes. For workers in the factory towns the pubs were the main source of pleasure and amusement from 6 a.m. to 11 p.m. Until the previous year they had been open all day on Sundays too, but a law had then been passed forbidding them to open until 12.30 p.m. and making them

A night with 'Old Tom' (gin) in a Victorian gin-palace

shut again in the afternoons. But it was still easy to get a Sunday morning drink, if you went round to the back door of a pub where your face was known. Or you could always go to the barber's shop for a 'morning rouser' of 'Old Tom' or the 'curse of Scotland' while you waited for a shave.

Bill went to neither gin palaces, singing saloons nor beerhouses. His 'regular'—the George and Dragon—was one of the better-class public houses in the district, where only tradesmen, shopkeepers and respectable working men were welcome. The downstairs windows and the panels in the doors were made of ornately engraved glass, as were the mirrors and the glass partitions inside. The bar counters and the shelves behind the bar were made of heavy, dark wood. The pub was always warm, clean and comfortable. There was a bottle and jug department, a snuggery and a general bar. Leading off the general bar there was a parlour for local shopkeepers and tradesmen and a coffee room, used by members of the various organizations which held their functions in the club room on the first floor.

A Day in the Life of a Victorian Factory Worker

Bill visited the pub at least once every week. Every other Friday night his friendly society held its meeting in the club room. The following week, on Saturday, his branch of the Amalgamated Society of Engineers also met there. He usually went on some other night too, as he could always have a joke and a chat with one of his mates, or a member of the Society 'on travel' who had come to find work in the town. They got their beer and bed and breakfast at the pub. The 'vacant book', which unemployed members of the Society had to sign every morning, and the 'box' from which they were paid their 'do', were also kept there. To prevent dishonesty, the box had three separate locks and keys kept by the president and two other officials of the branch. It was there, too, that many of the 'Saint Mondayites'—who preferred to treat the first working day of the week as a holiday—could be found drinking and playing dominoes in the morning, if the weather was too bad for them to take a cheap rail excursion to the seaside.

Bill ordered a pint of beer and looked around the room. In one corner a number of his mates were gathered round Bob Fossey, who had been 'on travel' to Loomtown several times before. Some members of the Society preferred to live a wandering life, moving round from town to town and living 'on the box' until they got a job. They kept the job for a few months, and then moved on again to another town. Because they knew all the interesting gossip about rates of pay, working conditions, employers and foremen in other parts of the country, they were always welcome visitors.

After filling his pipe from his tobacco box Bill went over to the group and sat down. Bob Fossey was one of their favourites; he always had a number of interesting and amusing stories to tell. In his time he had travelled all over England and Scotland. He knew the name of every 'slaughterhouse' where they worked you so hard that at the end of the day you were fit to drop, and of every shop where they 'horsed' men by making them race against each other on piecework. He had no respect for employers, whether they were millionaires or not, and called them 'Tom' instead of Mr Thomas Brown and 'Davy' instead of Mr David Robertson. He judged them solely on their merits as a man and their skills as an engineer. Everyone always said that if Bob Fossey had ever settled down he would have ended up as a manager or an employer himself, for there was no other fitter in the country who was more highly skilled. For that reason he never had any trouble in finding a job. He was just telling them how Davy Robertson had been prowling round his workshop one day, dressed like a labourer as usual, even though he was reputed to be a millionaire. He stood staring at a man who had just been engaged by the foreman that morning. After five or ten minutes the new man could stand it no longer and, thinking that Davy was a labourer, told him to get back to his work. He was 'on the box' again that afternoon.

54

Bill glanced up and saw that the man he had been waiting for had just come in. Tom White was a younger man who worked in Bill's own shop, and because he seemed to be a decent sort Bill had agreed to make him a member of his friendly society. Bill was just as careful in proposing members of the lodge as he was in recommending new members for his union, for the same reasons. As one of the 'sick stewards' of the lodge, Bill knew that there were already too many 'twisters' who claimed the sick benefit of 10s a week when they weren't entitled to it. But Tom White seemed to be an honest sort.

They went upstairs to the club room where the other members of the lodge were already assembled. When they reached the door Bill gave a secret knock —a complicated series of raps. A small slide in the door was opened from the inside. Bill whispered the password—'Brother Boddington without the word'—into someone's ear. They could hear murmuring from the room and then another distant voice saying, 'Admit Brother Boddington.'

Telling Tom White to wait outside, Bill went into the club room. He saluted the Noble Grand who sat at the far end of the room under a blue canopy. The Noble Grand wore a scarlet sash across his chest, and the other officers on either side of him also wore silk sashes of different colours—blue, crimson and gold. The room, which ran the whole length of the pub, contained two large tables at which nearly a hundred men were sitting, with their mugs of beer in front of them. The walls were covered with the flags, banners and mottoes of the lodge, and there was a large board with the names of past Noble Grands inscribed in gilt lettering.

After Bill had proposed that Tom White should be made a member, another man seconded him. The Noble Grand ordered him to be brought in. Bill went outside again and brought Tom White in and took him to the raised platform. There followed a short but impressive ceremony. After the Noble Grand had explained the purpose of the lodge, Tom White took an oath not to reveal its secrets. The members all rose and sang a special hymn about 'friendship and unity' before the Noble Grand made Tom White a member of the lodge. Then with raised glasses all the men gave a toast— 'Long life and happiness to our new brother, Tom White!'

Bill took Tom to a seat at one of the tables and whispered that it wouldn't be held against him if he ordered a gallon of beer, which Tom immediately did. The other business of the evening was quickly disposed of. Bill reported that Brother Smith had been seen drunk in the street and recommended that his sick pay should be stopped. The lodge agreed. The rest of the evening was devoted to the equally important business of drinking and talking. At 10 p.m. some of the men started to go home and by 11 p.m. the club room was empty.

The meetings of the friendly society and the union were Bill's major

A seaside scene in Victorian times

regular entertainments. The other weekly event he really looked forward to was his visit to the public baths. Every Saturday afternoon, with his second-best clothes over his arm, he walked into the town to visit the bath-house. The baths were situated in little cubicles off an iron gallery above the white-tiled swimming bath. There were first-class baths for gentlemen, and second-class baths, made of iron painted to look like marble, which he used. The water was always boiling hot and the towel, which was provided free, was always clean. The weekly bath always seemed to soak away all the tiredness and worries of the week, and he came out, clutching his bundle of dirty clothes, feeling completely refreshed and fit for the pleasures of the week-end.

He usually spent the rest of Saturday afternoon at home, pottering around the house or doing odd jobs, and once a fortnight he went to the union meeting in the evening. Now that he was a family man he couldn't afford to go out drinking every night at the week-end, or to visit the theatre or the music hall as he had done when he was a young man in London. During the summer, when the weather was fine, he would take the whole family for an excursion by train to the seaside on Sunday. They had been there three times that summer. He was always dressed in his best black suit, which he also used for funerals and marriages, while his wife wore her best Sunday bonnet and frock.

All the fun of the fair—with punch and judy, a dancing saloon, and the three-card trick

Sarah wore a pretty little frock of flowered cotton, decorated with frills and bows. And George looked splendid in his Sunday best outfit which they'd bought him that summer for special occasions—a Highland tunic with a black, glossy, leather belt and a large gilt clasp, tartan socks and a glengarry cap. They couldn't afford to buy a meal so they took their own sandwiches, bread and butter, buns and a packet of tea with them. They ate their food in a seaside tea garden, where a notice proclaimed: 'The kettle boiled for 2d a head'.

Apart from this, his only other entertainments during the year were the feasts provided by the 'footings' at the factory and the annual dinner of his friendly society's lodge. He also took a day off work for the two-day fair which was held in Loomtown every year. There was a circus and many side-shows with female giants, shooting galleries, bare-fisted pugilists, swings and gaily decorated roundabouts drawn by horses. The stalls displayed all kinds of delicious food: gingerbread, brandysnaps, pies, black pudding, cakes and Californian peas. He also took an unpaid holiday of two or three days at Christmas, Whitsun and Easter, which he had done even before Bank Holidays had been started two years before.

While Bill had been enjoying his night out at the lodge, Mrs Boddington had been working. After she put the children to bed and washed up, she kneaded the dough and put it in the baking tins to rise again. Although it was scarcely any cheaper to make bread at home, she usually made some when they were having relatives in. Her younger sister and her husband—who also worked in a factory—and their three children, were coming round for Sunday dinner. This was their main meal of the week, when Mrs Boddington got out her best tablecloth and the best set of knives and forks; these had been given to her as a wedding present and were kept carefully wrapped up among the linen during the rest of the week. She had already planned what they would have: a leg of mutton with onions, cabbage and potatoes, followed by a rabbit pie, and the Nun's pudding that they all liked, made of breadcrumbs, sugar, eggs and milk. There would also be home-made bread and cheese for the men if they wanted it, and beer for them, and tea for her sister and herself and the children.

As the kitchen table wasn't big enough she would bring down the table and chairs and a few boxes from the bedroom so that the children could eat in the scullery. It would be different when she had moved into her new home. After the meal she and her sister would go into the scullery too, to wash up and to keep the children quiet while the men chatted by the fire or had forty winks.

While Mrs Boddington was waiting for the bread to rise she got out some socks and started darning them on a wooden 'mushroom'. She sat there quietly by the light of the oil lamp waiting for Bill to return. After a while she got up and put the tins in the oven. It wouldn't be long before he came home. She sat by the fire, darning patiently, waiting for the bread to bake and for her husband to return. Another day had passed.

7. *THE NATIONAL SCENE*

Bill Boddington lived and worked in the period when Britain was at the peak of its power. In the mid-Victorian age visitors from all parts of the world, including the United States, were astonished by the vast wealth of the manufacturers and the huge factories in the northern towns. No other country in the world had anything to compare with it, as Britain had gained a start over all other nations in the development of industry. During the last quarter of the eighteenth century, the first spinning mills were built on the banks of fast-flowing rivers in the lonely valleys of the north. The machinery was driven by water wheels and much of the work was done by little children who had been apprenticed from the workhouses at the age of seven or eight.

After James Watt had invented a steam engine in 1781 which could drive the wheels of machinery, the spinning mills no longer had to depend on the rivers as a source of power and could be built in the existing towns. Only the spinning of cotton was done in factories; the weaving of the cloth was still done in the weaver's own home on a hand loom. But once machinery for weaving cotton had been perfected at the beginning of the nineteenth century, power looms were also installed in the factories. The whole process of making cloth which had once been carried out in the workers' own homes was now done in factories. As more and more people moved into the towns to work in the mills the outlines of the huge industrial towns of the present day started to take shape. The process was well advanced by the 1820s.

'The town of Manchester has, from an unimportant provincial town, become the second in extent and population in England, and Liverpool has become in opulence, magnitude, elegance and commerce, the second Seaport in Europe. That Liverpool is a consequence of the Cotton Manufacture, and indebted to Manchester and its dependencies for its greatness, is evident . . . The origin of a Manufacturing Town is this: a Manufactory is established, a number of labourers and artisans are collected—these have wants which must be supplied by the Corn Dealer, the Butcher, the Builder, the Shopkeeper—the latter when added to the Colony have themselves need of the Draper, the Grocer, etc. Fresh multitudes of every various trade and business, whether conducive to the wants or luxury of

One of the early cotton mills in Lancashire

the inhabitants, are superadded, and thus is the Manufacturing town formed.'[1]

The textile industry was the first to be mechanized and was for many years the mainstay of Britain's prosperity. The cheap cotton cloth found a ready market in all parts of the world, particularly in Africa, Latin America and the East. Between 1815 and the middle of the nineteenth century, almost half of the value of Britain's exports came from cotton. But there were also developments in other industries. The increasing use of steam engines and the growth of population in towns stimulated the demand for coal. This in its turn made it necessary to find a more efficient means of transporting it than by packhorses and wagons. Canals were built but these were quickly superseded by railways, with steam locomotives pulling freight wagons and passenger coaches. The growth of the railway system stimulated the demand for coal even further. The increasing use of machinery in factories and on the railways meant that new and more efficient means of making iron had to be found and that even more factories had to be set up to build locomotives, steam engines and textile machinery. The industrial revolution was a cumulative process which extended over many years.

By the time Bill Boddington started work in 1852, Britain was the leading industrial nation in the world. According to one recent estimate it produced about two-thirds of the world's coal—then its main source of industrial fuel— about half the iron and factory-made cotton cloth, and nearly half (in value) of its hardware.[2] Its textiles, its locomotives, its ships were renowned all over the world. The phrase 'made in Britain' was a guarantee of good workman-ship, high quality and low cost. At about that time, the factory methods of production which had been so successfully applied to the textile industries started to be used in other trades and industries. Individual towns and districts became famous throughout the world for particular products. Wolverhamp-ton and its surrounding district acquired a high reputation for the locks and other metal goods it produced. At John Harper's works at Willenhall, a cheap, ornamental door lock, which cost $7\frac{1}{2}$d, was manufactured mainly for the Canadian and American markets, while a tumbler padlock was sold 'in prodigious quantities in the East, and stands unrivalled for cheapness and simplicity, seeing that it can be sold in retail for 1d each'.[3] British hand-made goods were equally esteemed throughout the world. Sheffield, for example, was well known for its cutlery—highly polished silver and electro-plated spoons and forks, and knives with a sharp cutting edge and handles made

[1] Richard Guest, *A Compendious History of the Cotton Manufacture*, Manchester, 1823, p. 4.
[2] Cf. E. J. Hobsbawm, 'Industry and Empire', *The Pelican Economic History of Britain*, Penguin, 1969, vol. 3, p. 134.
[3] Dr G. L. M. Strauss *et. al.*, *England's Workshops*, London, 1864, p. 128.

Grinding blades for table knives by hand

of silver, real ivory or mother of pearl. Their reputation was so high that many American and Continental manufacturers made imitations and foisted 'their worthless rubbish upon the public abroad by forging the name and trade mark and imitating the labels and packages of eminent Sheffield firms, like Messrs Mappin, Rodgers, Wolstenholm and many others'.[1]

The rapid development of industry brought vast fortunes to many manufacturers and factory owners. Some of them, like Sir Richard Arkwright, came from poor families. The youngest of a family of thirteen children, he started life as a barber, but in 1771 opened the first of his water-powered cotton mills at Cromford, Derbyshire. By the time he died in 1792, he had a share in a whole chain of mills in various parts of the country and had made a fortune of £500,000. Other manufacturers came from old-established county families, like the Ormrods of Lancashire who had been granted lands near Burnley in the thirteenth century. One of the descendants, Peter Ormrod, who was born in 1795, became a partner in a cotton-spinning mill. He became so wealthy that just before his death in 1875 he gave £45,000 for the building of a new parish church in Bolton; it was to replace the old one whose fabric had been rotted by the smoke and grime of the polluted air.[2]

In Victorian Britain the rich were very rich and the poor were very poor.

[1] Ibid., p. 111.
[2] Cf. James Clegg, *Annals of Bolton*, Bolton, 1888, p. 148.

According to one estimate made in 1867, there were 7,500 people in England and Wales—including 350 companies which were each treated as one person for income tax purposes—with an income over £5,000 a year, and another 42,000 with an income between £1,000 and £5,000 a year.[1] (These were enormous incomes by present-day standards, as prices were much lower and income tax, which had been reintroduced by Sir Robert Peel in 1842 at 7d in the pound, had fallen to 2d in the pound by 1874.) At the same time, very few manual workers, apart from foremen, had an income of £100 a year, and most of them earned considerably less. The highest average weekly wage of 35s a week went to engine drivers and to makers of scientific, surgical and optical instruments, scales, leather cases, watches and jewellery. Fitters came into the third category of workers earning 25s a week—with warehousemen, coachmakers, and blacksmiths.[2] But between about 1867 and 1875 the wages of practically all manual workers rose—perhaps by 20 per cent. By 1875, according to one contemporary report, fitters in four Manchester factories were receiving up to 38s a week while some smiths were earning £2 a week.[3] These increases brought stern moral warnings from the middle classes about how the workers should spend their newly acquired 'wealth':

'A sudden increase of wages, as in the colliery districts in 1872–73, may find the recipients utterly unprepared for their good fortune. And so we have heard of miners indulging in Champagne wine, and of puddlers purchasing for themselves sealskin waistcoats. But reason speedily asserts her higher sway. The housewife eagerly arrests a portion of the higher wages to furnish the bare rooms, to fill the empty cupboard, and to clothe the children. Little by little as the novel condition with its bountiful stores is realized, self-respect increases, sobriety of conduct is induced, and the family as a whole rises to habits of virtue and propriety.'[4]

But their 'good fortune' was greatly exaggerated. Workers' wages then left little room for luxuries or indulgence, even in the case of a skilled man like Bill Boddington, who was among the 'aristocrats' of the working classes. Nevertheless there was some variation in the way the skilled workers spent their wages. Some men, like Samuel Cousins, were 'lushingtons'; most of their wages went straight into the pockets of the brewers. Others, like Bill Boddington and his wife, managed their money more carefully. As one contemporary engineer pointed out: 'There is no typical working man . . .

[1] Cf. R. Dudley Baxter, *National Income, The United Kingdom*, Macmillan, 1868, p. 36.
[2] Cf. Ibid., p. 90.
[3] G. Phillips Bevan, *The Industrial Classes and Industrial Statistics*, London, 1876, p. 117.
[4] Sir Leone Levi, *Wages and Earnings of the Working Classes*, London, 1885, p. 16.

There is an educated and really intelligent section; a political section (broken up again into several sub-sections) and a non-political section; a trade unionist and a non-trade unionist section; a sober, steady, saving section, and a drunken, unsteady, thriftless section.'[1]

Bill Boddington belonged to the educated, non-political, trade unionist, sober sections. He was much better off than the unskilled workers in the factory, mainly because he had a strong union to protect him. The Amalgamated Society of Engineers, formed out of a number of existing unions in 1851, was the first of the 'new model' unions, with headquarters in London, an efficient leadership and adequate financial resources. By the end of 1870 its membership had increased from the original 7,000 to 34,711 members, with branches in all the main engineering centres at home and some branches abroad. Manchester, for example, had nine branches in 1870, with 100 to 290 members each.[2] The union, with its high subscription rate, was designed to exclude the unskilled and to protect the privileges of members. Any member who obtained work for a non-Society man without the permission of branch officials could, under a union rule of 1864, be fined at least 5s.[3] The union was anything but radical. Just after it was formed, the union protested against enforced overtime, piecework and unskilled men working on the machines, which resulted in a four-month lock-out by the employers. The union capitulated and there were no really major strikes for another twenty years, until the Newcastle and Sunderland members went on strike for a nine-hour day in 1871. This was followed by a number of unofficial strikes in various places by more militant members who had become disillusioned with the rather conservative leadership.

Although skilled and unskilled workers often lived side by side in the same street or court, the craftsman, particularly if he had older children at work or only a small family, could live very much better than his unskilled neighbour. Their higher wages gave them bigger opportunities to secure better living accommodation. Some of the 'sober, steady, saving section', like Bill Boddington, could even afford to buy a cheap terrace house of their own, with a small garden, a backyard, gas lighting and a separate privy, or even a water closet. Or he could afford to move into one of the 'model' blocks of flats, built in some large towns by such philanthropic organizations as the Peabody Trust, set up by an American merchant, George Peabody, or the Improved Industrial Dwellings Company, established by Sir Sydney Waterlow, one-time Lord Mayor of London. These blocks of flats, four or

[1] Thomas Wright, *Our New Masters*, London, 1873, pp. 5–6.
[2] Cf. General Secretary's remarks, *Twentieth Annual Report of the Amalgamated Society of Engineers, Machinists, Millwrights, Smiths and Pattern Makers*, London, 1871.
[3] Cf. William Allan, Secretary of the A.S.E., *Evidence to Royal Commission on Trade Unions*, Parliamentary Papers, London, 1867, vol. 32, p. 36.

five storeys high, had balconies with iron balustrades, water closets, sinks and coppers. The rents were usually too high for anyone but a craftsman to afford. In Langbourne Buildings, Finsbury Square, London, for example, they ranged from 5s to 7s 6d a week.

But very few workers had such good accommodation. Water closets were exceptional in working-class homes and remained so for many years. Even some housing reformers, like James Hole of Leeds, were opposed to them, mainly because he felt that the working classes would not be able to afford to keep them in good order, and because he doubted if it would be possible to provide the larger supplies of water required.[1] The pail or the ashpit was the usual form of sanitation in working-class homes; it was often shared with several other families. The pails were collected during the day in many large towns. In 1873 collections were made in Rochdale between 7 a.m. and 5.30 p.m., while Hull, with more modesty, made its collections between 5 and 8.30 a.m. in the summer and 6 and 9.30 a.m. in the winter.[2] It was not until the end of the nineteenth century that some large cities, like Glasgow, started to replace privies by water closets and 'Nottingham as late as 1908 had 10,000 more pail closets than water closets'.[3]

Gas lighting was also exceptional in working-class homes before the end of the nineteenth century, though it did exist in some. By the middle of the century it had become common in some upper-class and middle-class houses. The gas came straight out of the burner and burnt with a yellowish, smoky light; it was not until 1893 that an incandescent gas mantle, which gave a brighter, whiter light, was introduced.[4] Until the end of the century most working-class homes had to make do with candles and oil lamps, which burnt paraffin from about 1860 instead of colza oil made from rape seed.[5]

The higher wages of the skilled worker also gave him a bigger choice in the kind of school to which he could send his children. Before the passing of the Education Act of 1870, there were a small number of schools in some of the large industrial towns which were patronized only by the children of small shopkeepers and skilled artisans, as the fees were high, ranging from 6s to 12s a quarter.[6] Most of the large, government-inspected schools in

[1] Cf. James Hole, *The Homes of the Working Classes, with Suggestions for their Improvement*, Longman, Green, 1866, pp. 152–3.
[2] Report by Mr J. Netten Radcliffe, 'Certain Means of Preventing Excrement Nuisances in Towns and Villages', *Reports of the Medical Officer of the Privy Council and Local Government Board*, Parliamentary Papers, London, 1874, vol. 31, Appendix 7, pp. 159 and 174.
[3] Geoffrey Best, *Mid-Victorian Britain, 1851–1875*, Weidenfeld and Nicolson, 1971, p. 23.
[4] Cf. F. W. Robins, *The Story of the Lamp (and the Candle)*, Oxford University Press, 1939, p. 119.
[5] Cf. Ibid., p. 114.
[6] Cf. *Report on Schools for Poorer Classes in Birmingham, Leeds, Liverpool and Manchester*, Appendix to Mr Fearon's Report, Parliamentary Papers, London, 1870, vol. 54, p. 397.

Manchester and Liverpool (apart from the Roman Catholic schools in Liverpool) did not admit children of the lowest labouring classes, as the children of skilled workers would have been taken away.[1] Labourers' children went to other, less exclusive schools, which were often also attended by children working part-time in mills and factories. Under the Factory Acts such children were obliged to have some education; many of them had never been to school until they started work in the factory at the age of ten or eleven. The poorest children went to 'ragged' schools, or none at all. There were also private 'adventure' schools, which provided no adventure for the pupils but a profitable commercial venture for the dames who ran them.

This situation did not change immediately after the 1870 Education Act was passed. The Act made it necessary for an elected School Board to be set up where the provision of education was not considered to be efficient. School Boards were established in most of the big industrial towns. A massive building programme was instituted with some existing schools being taken over and temporary accommodation being provided while the new Board schools were being built. Uniformity in attendance was not achieved for many years. The Act allowed the Boards to grant exemption to children from the age of ten for the whole or part of the day. The practice of Boards varied from town to town. Bolton, for example, gave exemption from the age of ten if children had passed the Standard Six examination, while in Salford they were exempted if they had passed Standard Four.[2] As the new school attendance officers started to force the reluctant children of poorer parents into the Board schools, those schools which charged higher fees enjoyed a boom as did also some of the 'adventure' schools, because, as some mothers said, the children 'don't get infectious diseases' and 'don't get so rough' there.[3] Respectability remained a bigger criterion than educational progress. Not all skilled workers sent their children to the dearest schools. An inquiry made in Sheffield in 1875 showed that well over half of 400 parents with children in 'ragged' schools—where the fees were 1d a week—were skilled workers.[4]

The skilled worker with his higher wages was also able to eat better than his unskilled neighbour. Those who managed their money well could afford to have meat on most days—roast leg of mutton, hashed mutton, rissoles, mutton pie, Irish stew, boiled sheep's head with lights, steak pie or tripe and

---

[1] Cf. Ibid., p. 446.
[2] Cf. *Reports of Her Majesty's Inspectors, E. H. Brodie in the County of Lancaster*, Parliamentary Papers, London, 1873, vol. 24, p. 56.
[3] Ibid., p. 55.
[4] Cf. J. H. Bingham, *The Period of the Sheffield School Board, 1870–1903*, Sheffield, 1949, p. 65.

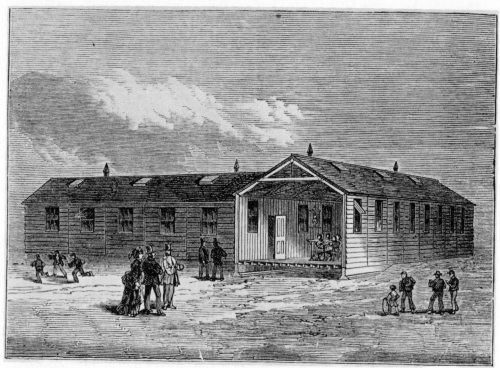

Temporary classrooms are nothing new. In the 1870s many school boards were forced to put up movable schools to cope with the inrush of children

onions. The main meal of the week was at Sunday dinnertime when there would often be meat and a pie of some kind, followed by a pudding (rice, bread and butter, or Nun's) or pancakes.[1]

On the whole, however, the way of life of Bill Boddington and other skilled craftsmen like him was very modest by today's standards. Illness, continued unemployment, or extravagance of any kind was enough to reduce a family to penury. Even when they were in regular employment, such things as mass-produced bedroom suites, which cost over £3, or better-quality bedroom suites in satinwood or oak, costing from £10 upwards, and upright pianos at £30 were usually far outside the reach of even the most prosperous of the working classes—the 1,000,000 or more skilled workers. They were even further beyond the reach of the 3,819,000 'lower skilled labour' class and the 2,843,000 unskilled and agricultural workers.[2]

The gap between the skilled and the unskilled workers, as contemporary writers were agreed, was very great. 'There is, for example, in these two

[1] Cf. Marian Smithard, *Cookery for the Artisan and Others*, Chapman and Hall, 1878, *passim*.
[2] Cf. Baxter, op. cit., p. 51.

boroughs [Manchester and Liverpool] a much wider gulf between the unskilled and skilled labour, than that which exists between the skilled labourer, and a person [such as a small shopkeeper] low down in the scale of middle-class society.'[1] In the 1870s, the unskilled factory worker earned about £1 a week. His wages were scarcely sufficient to support a family, unless his wife or his older children were also working. His wife patronized the cheapest shops and was often forced to visit the pawnbroker on Monday to borrow money on her husband's one decent suit or the blankets, which she redeemed on the following Friday after her husband had been paid. The unskilled labourer did the hardest, dirtiest and most boring work, wielding a sledgehammer or lifting, carrying and fetching things for a skilled man. If the craftsman decided to stay away from work on 'Saint Monday', there was no work—or pay—for the unskilled labourer who assisted him. When there was a strike—in which the unskilled man had no voice—he was made idle too, with no union strike pay to help him. If he was injured he received no sick pay, and when he was too old to work only the bleak misery of the workhouse awaited him—and his family.[2]

Below the unskilled labourer there was another class—the really desperate poor who had sunk so low that begging, crime or the workhouse was their only salvation. Any worker who was unlucky enough to fall seriously ill or to be unemployed for long, could quickly fall into this state. A minority of the Victorian middle class were fully conscious of the social problem of the poor:

'Those who need assurance of the hunger of hundreds of their poor neighbours need not go very far to obtain it. A quarter of an hour at the window of any common cook-shop in a "low neighbourhood", at about seven o'clock in the evening, when the steam of . . . puddings is blurring the glass, and the odour of leg-of-beef soup and pease-pudding comes in gusts to the chilly street should suffice. There is pretty sure to be a group of poor little eager-eyed, pinch-nosed boys and girls peering wistfully in to watch the fortunate possessor of 2d who comes out with something smoking hot on a cabbage leaf . . .'[3]

Although charitable organizations were set up, they could deal only with the fringes of this vast problem. Sometimes, they seemed more concerned to stamp out abuse of their charity—which certainly did exist—than

[1] *Reports on Schools for Poorer Classes*, op. cit., p. 441.
[2] Cf. 'A Working Man', *Working Men and Women*, London, 1867, pp. 105 *et. seq.*
[3] Thomas Archer, 'About my Father's Business', *Work Amidst the Sick, the Sad, and the Sorrowing*, London, 1876, p. 210.

to relieve suffering. Two cases which found no sympathy at the Bethnal Green were:

'UNDESERVING

Case 1,206.—This is a case of a man aged thirty-one, deaf and dumb. Application for help or employment. Inquiry proved this man to be an imposter; he had been living almost entirely by begging during the past two years. The applicant acknowledged that he gets as much as 4s or 5s per day. He is also given to drink and was discharged from last situation through getting drunk.

Case 1,353.—A man and wife and six children—the man a jeweller, aged thirty-five. Statement of wife: "My work as a machinist is very slack. If I could get a machine I could have work at once. My husband is a working jeweller, but has had very little work during the past two years." . . . Inquiry proved the man to be a drunkard and a blackguard . . . The woman is sober, but a bad principle, and never pays anybody.'[1]

Too often, middle-class Victorians blamed drink for the cause of poverty, even though it was more often a symptom of the person's despair than the cause. There were thousands of cases of genuine distress, for which drink could not be blamed, of which the following is just one example:

'John Little was even nearer starvation . . . He lived with Mrs Little in a small, third-floor back room . . . I saw that they were very poor, as they had no bed, though they had two chairs and a table. They never asked for anything, and as I often found him cobbling, I did not guess what a state of destitution he was in . . . However, one cold day in February, I found this man unable to work and looking very ill. I suspected it was from want of food, so I got him some at once. The next day I found him much worse and I fetched the clergyman to him and sent for the parish doctor, leaving money and food with him. An hour after I had left the house Little broke a blood vessel in the stomach, and was taken in a cab to the nearest hospital. There they said they would not receive him, so he was brought back home. Ice had been applied, but he was still losing blood, and in this condition he was dragged up again to the third-floor room.'[2]

Eventually he was taken to the workhouse hospital, where he recovered. Although there were these great distinctions between the skilled crafts-

[1] Society for Organising Charitable Relief and Repressing Mendacity, Bethnal Committee, *Fifth Annual Report, 1874–5*, Bethnal Green, 1875.
[2] Anon., *Work About the Five Dials*, Macmillan, 1878, pp. 14–15.

Drinking fountains were one of the great
contributions to better public health in
the Victorian age

man, the unskilled labourer, and the really poor in the industrial towns of
the 1870s, they were all subject to some common deprivations. The towns
in which they lived and worked were ugly, bleak, unhealthy places, in spite
of the improvements which had been made in the previous thirty years by
providing better water supplies, paving roads and opening public parks.
In fact, in some ways conditions had worsened during that period, because
of the great growth of industry. 'The inhabitant whose memory can carry
him back thirty years [i.e. to 1836], recalls pictures of rural beauty, suburban
mansions and farmsteads, green fields, waving trees, and clear streams where
fish could live—where now can be seen only streets, factories and workshops,
and a river or brook black as the ink which now runs from our pen describing
it!'[1]

As a consequence of this spread of industry the middle classes started
to move out of the city to suburban villas two or three miles away, thus
increasing the physical separation of the classes. Existing middle-class
homes were razed to the ground to make way for factories or large stores,
or split up into tenements with the poorest families living in one room in the

[1] Hole, op. cit., p. 3.

cellar, for which they paid a rent of 1s or 1s 6d a week. Living conditions in the centres of towns started to deteriorate rapidly, as large houses and their gardens were bought up and speculators built back-to-back houses in their place. Some towns, like Manchester, banned the building of back-to-back houses as early as 1844, and made it compulsory for all houses to have a backyard of their own. But such local by-laws were frequently ignored. The government tried to persuade local authorities to close insanitary houses in their area by passing the Artisans' and Labourers' Dwellings Act of 1868; but because it cost so much to compensate the owners few councils took advantage of this chance. Further laws passed in the 1870s and the 1880s gave local authorities powers of compulsory purchase to clear whole areas of slums but, again, action was seldom taken.

In the poorer areas of the towns around the factories, where the skilled and unskilled often lived as neighbours, there were still commonly unpaved streets, inadequate water supplies with only a standpipe to supply a whole row of houses, and shared sanitation. One consequence of these poor living conditions was that the death rate among all workers was very high. Although engineering was not a particularly unhealthy trade, the average age of death of members of the Amalgamated Society of Engineers between 1860 and 1870 was thirty-seven and a half. By 1885–9 the average age of death had risen to forty-eight, mainly because of better living conditions and improvements in medical science.[1]

Working conditions in factories remained in many ways as bad as housing conditions. The worst forms of exploitation in factories and mines had been ended by the Factory Act of 1833, which restricted young children's hours of work to nine a day, and the Mines Act of 1842 which prohibited women and children from working underground in coal mines. But hours of work remained long. It was not until 1874 that the law gave women and young persons a ten-hour working day in factories, though most engineers had obtained a nine-hour day through agreement between union and employers a few years before that. But the necessity to work overtime meant in practice that many of them continued to work a sixty-hour week. Many factories of all kinds were poorly-ventilated, dark and dangerous places. Accidents were very common. The total number of serious accidents reported in six months of 1872 was 3,823.[2] Even after the Factory Act of 1878 had provided that there should be safety guards on dangerous machinery, the regulation was often ignored as there were so few factory inspectors to see that it was carried out.

Conditions in many small workshops were even worse than they were in

[1] Cf. James B. Jefferys, *The Story of the Engineers, 1800–1945*, Lawrence and Wishart, n.d., p. 66.
[2] Cf. *Reports of the Inspector of Factories for the half year ending 31 October 1872*, London, 1873, p. 4.

factories. It is not accurately known how many people were employed in workshops. But even by the end of the nineteenth century, according to one very detailed contemporary estimate, almost a quarter of the 5 million people working in industry were employed in small workshops with less than ten workers. There were still relatively few large factories employing more than 1,000 people—65 in the textile industry and 128 in other trades.[1]

During the Great Depression of 1873–96, when prices and profits fell in all countries, Britain lost the place it had once held as the 'workshop of the world'. It was overtaken by the United States and Germany in many spheres—technology, training, production and working methods. In Britain the period from 1850 to 1890 saw few technical advances in the engineering industry. Centre lathes and planers remained the chief machines and much of the fitters' work was still done by hand—with chisels, files and scrapers.[2] In the 1860s many firms were still producing engineering goods of all kinds; machine tools, steam hammers, steam engines, boilers, steam cranes and equipment for the gas industry were among the numerous products of one London firm.[3] But from the 1870s many engineering firms started to specialize.

Although the Great Depression saw the beginning of the end of Britain as a great power, it was a period of much greater prosperity for the working classes. Not only did their wages rise, particularly from about the middle of the 1880s, but prices fell dramatically, particularly those of imported food and manufactured goods. Goods which had once been unobtainable luxuries—pianos, linoleum, sewing machines—started to come within the budgets of the more affluent members of the working classes. Clothes, too, could be bought in greater quantities, as the mass production of boots and shoes and then of suits became more common. Eating patterns also changed with the introduction of cheap jam, fish and chips, margarine and cheaper meat from Latin America. Newspapers and magazines became cheaper; the first popular $\frac{1}{2}$d daily national newspaper, the *Daily Mail*, appeared in 1896. Cheap workmen's fares on many railways and the introduction of horse-drawn trams from the 1860s and electric trams from 1900, made it easier for the working classes to live further away from their place of work. The pub remained a popular form of entertainment, but with the new licensing laws of 1872 and 1874 which restricted the hours of opening, and the increasing availability of other goods, consumption of beer—the working man's main drink—started to decline. The amount drunk fell from 36

---

[1] Cf. P. Kropotkin, *Fields, Factories and Workshops*, Thomas Nelson, n.d., pp. 253–84.
[2] Cf. Jefferys, op. cit., pp. 122–4.
[3] Cf. *Descriptive List for the Year 1864 of General Machinery Manufactured by G. Buchanan & Co., London, E.C.*, London, n.d.

gallons per head of the population in 1876 to 27 gallons by 1883.[1] The working man turned to other forms of amusement—the music hall and that unique working-class contribution to the world of entertainment, Soccer.

The modern game had been introduced at public schools and Cambridge University in the middle of the nineteenth century. Until the 1880s it was still an amateur game, with the players wearing long trousers and caps and the teams changing sides every time a goal was scored. The first Cup Final at the Oval in 1872 was watched by only 2,000 spectators, but by the end of the century the game had become a major Saturday-afternoon entertainment, and the Cup Final was attracting crowds of 80,000 or more. Professionals took over after the Football League was formed in 1888. The original twelve clubs were: Preston North End, Aston Villa, Wolverhampton Wanderers, Blackburn Rovers, Bolton Wanderers, West Bromwich Albion, Accrington, Everton, Burnley, Derby County, Notts County and Stoke.[2] As Hobsbawm has said, 'Between 1870 and 1900 the pattern of British working-class life which the writers, dramatists, and T.V. producers of the 1950s thought of as "traditional" came into being.'[3]

But it was mainly the skilled workers who benefited by these developments. Research by Charles Booth in London and Seebohm Rowntree in York showed that at the end of the nineteenth century something like one-third of the population were still living below the poverty line. Their condition did not improve up to the First World War, as from 1900 prices started to rise again.

Between the two world wars, the staple industries of textiles, iron and steel, shipbuilding and coalmining continued to decline, resulting in massive unemployment which rose to just under 3 million in 1932. But outside the depressed areas, there was increased prosperity and industrial development. From the early 1920s, the mass-production methods which had been pioneered by Henry Ford in the United States were applied to the British car industry in the Midlands. And in the south, particularly in the London area, many new factories were opened in the middle of the depression to produce new goods—radios, vacuum cleaners, plastics. The standard of living of the skilled worker who retained his job again rose during this period, but many of the features of the older way of life still remained.

It is only since the 1950s that the lives of most factory workers have been improved out of all recognition. The unions which were once a means of retaining privileges for the skilled, now cover workers of all grades. As a consequence, the gap in wages between the skilled and the unskilled has

[1] Cf. Levi, op. cit., p. 26.
[2] Cf. Geoffrey Green, *Soccer: The World Game, A Popular History*, Phoenix House, 1953, p. 53.
[3] Hobsbawm, op. cit., p. 164.

Public laundries, which were first opened in the early years of Victoria's reign, continued to be used right up to the time when the modern laundrette was introduced. This photograph was taken in London in 1931

narrowed greatly. New materials, such as plastics, and new techniques, such as automation, have brought about fundamental changes in factory work. The modern engineer is much more highly skilled than his mid-Victorian counterpart. Bill Boddington, or even his father, would have been quite at home in an engineering shop in the 1890s. Today they would only be allowed to sweep the floors.

But some features of the earlier period still remain. Although wages are much higher, many workers are still forced to do overtime to bring their take-home pay up to a reasonable level. Unskilled workers no longer need great physical strength to do their jobs, as machines, such as fork-lift trucks, have taken much of the hard labour out of their work. But much unskilled work still remains boring and undemanding—picking skins out of chopped onions in a pickle factory, assembling components in an electronics factory. Far too many of the old terrace houses, which were unfit for human habitation even when they were built, are still occupied. The legacy of the past still lies heavily on many factory towns, but the outlines of a new, cleaner, wealthier life is beginning to emerge.

Appendix

There are many different ways in which the material in this book can be followed up at the local level. The story of Bill Boddington and his family is all based on authentic material, but there were considerable variations in the living conditions of factory workers from town to town. These local variations in such fields as education, sanitation, housing and the development of industry can all be profitably studied. The development of education, for example, can be investigated in the minute books of education authorities and in the log books of schools, which are often preserved in local record offices. The rate of industrial growth in a town can be studied in the rate books, which are also often to be found in the record office, and by comparing old Ordnance survey maps and old directories, which are sometimes available in public libraries.

On-the-spot investigations of the physical remains of the past are particularly rewarding. Most industrial towns still have old factories and working-class homes from this period, waiting to be explored, studied, sketched, or photographed. A helpful series—The Industrial Archaeology of the British Isles—has been published by David and Charles: Owen Ashmore has contributed a valuable volume on Lancashire (*The Industrial Archaeology of Lancashire*, David and Charles, 1969) which has a comprehensive, descriptive gazetteer of the sites of old mills, factories, houses, railways, etc.

It is unnecessary to confine research projects to urban variations. There is still much work to be done on the class structure of Victorian Britain, in which local history can play a major part. There is a mass of unexplored documentation on the really poor in the local records of charity organizations, Boards of Guardians, poor law schools, etc., some of which may be found in record offices.

The development in time of some of the features of working class and factory life described in this book might be one of the most useful and rewarding projects. Histories of local firms, of mechanics' institutes, of trade unions in the area—where they exist—provide good starting points. But a more original means of study might be through individual or group interviews with living witnesses of the past. Memories of industrial and social conditions can take us back almost to the beginning of the century. Reminiscences of older people might be tape-recorded or written down, and then discussed in a group. Even though these memories may need to be substantiated elsewhere before they can be accepted as historical evidence, they often provide vivid detail of the past which cannot be obtained in any other way.

For further reading

G. A. Chinnery, *Studying Urban History in Schools*, Teaching of History Pamphlets, No. 33, Historical Association, London.

W. N. Chaloner, *The Skilled Artisans during the Industrial Revolution, 1750–1850*, Aids for Teachers, Historical Association, London.

T. K. Derry and Trevor I. Williams, *A Short History of Technology from the Earliest Times to A.D. 1900*, Oxford University Press, 1960.

Robert Douch, *Local History and the Teacher*, Routledge and Kegan Paul, 1967.

Ursula Henriques, *The Early Factory Acts and their Enforcement*, Appreciations in History, No. 1, Historical Association, London, 1971.

Frank E. Huggett, *Factory Life and Work*, Harrap, 1973.

Index